# Meditations in the Evening

*"When I remember you on my bed, I meditate on you in the night watches."*

**Psalm 63:6 NKJV**

By

Danny G. Thomas

FWB
For Worthwhile Books Publications
Columbus, Ohio

# Table of Contents

# Introduction

*"Therefore, since we are surrounded by so great a cloud of witnesses, let us also lay aside every weight, and sin which clings so closely, and let us run with endurance the race that is set before us, looking unto Jesus the founder and perfecter of our faith, who for the joy that was set before him endured the cross, despising the shame, and is seated at the right hand of the throne of God."* **Hebrews 12:1-2 ESV**

Have you ever thought of those people that God has placed in your life? Have you ever taken a moment to think about how you think, the way you see things, what it is that makes you happy or sad? If you know Jesus Christ as your Savior, then someone lived a life before you who encouraged and challenged you to consider His great love. Who was that person? Who were those people?

What are your goals in life? What do you like to do on weekends? What type of car do you drive? Did you finish high school, did you go to college, trade school or were you perhaps mentored in some trade or profession? Who was it that led you to make those choices and life changing decisions? Who set those skills that you have and shaped the thoughts and the knowledge you have?

I can think of many other similar questions but you get the idea. You are what you are because of the people who have been placed into your life - those special people who made you think or did the thinking for you; those people who challenged you. Who were those people?

The writer of Hebrews tells of a great crowd of witnesses that line the coliseum of Heaven who are cheering us on in the race that is set before us. The Apostle Paul reminds Timothy of his grandmother Lois and his mother Eunice who shaped his young life. **2 Timothy 1:5**

I want you to understand that each person in your life makes a difference. It really does matter whom you are around and who your friends are. You may be unaware of it, but your life matters to people, too. You make a difference in their lives. What you do, the things that you say, the places where you go, even the things that you think and what you watch matter. Each of those things (what you say, where you go, or watch) is shaping your life, and there are those who are watching you. It matters to them. You may be unaware of it, but there are those who know you and look up to you, and you are shaping them right now.

I think Satan would not want you to know that. He is totally OKAY with you thinking that you are unimportant and of little value to anyone, but that is a lie. You are extremely important and of great value. You need to know it. You also need to understand that among those who have helped shape you, some wanted you to be successful, and then there were those who used you, took advantage of you, and wanted you to fail. They helped shape you also.

The purpose of this book is to cause you to think: think about people, events, and situations that God has allowed in your life. Think about them and see God's hand in them. Sit back and think. Think about them and how God has worked and fitted things all together.

*"When I remember you upon my bed, and meditate on You in the watches of the night; for you have been my help, and in the shadow of your wings I will sing for joy. My soul clings to you; your right hand upholds me."* **Psalm 63:6 ESV**

How marvelous are Your ways O Lord, and mighty are Your works, how precious are Your thoughts toward me! **Psalm 139:17**

Think about that. *Selah!*

**Day 1:  Jesus Christ:** *Founder and Perfecter of our Faith*

*"Looking unto Jesus, the author and finisher of our faith; who for the joy that was set before him endured the cross, despising the shame, and is set down at the right hand of the throne of God."* **Hebrews 12:2 KJV**

Jesus Christ is the only begotten Son of God.  The very reason He came to earth was to make a positive impact on as many as would receive Him.  He did not come into this world to condemn this world, though that is what is often preached from pulpits all over this world. He came to save.  We were already condemned.

Jesus is the Savior and He came to save the people of the world from the curse of sin in their lives and to free them from sin's penalty.  You see, the world was already lost, already condemned before Jesus came and way before He was born in Bethlehem.  The angels of heaven proclaimed it to the shepherds that were out in the field on the night of His birth.  They told those shepherds that there was a *Savior* who was born that night who was none other than the Messiah, the Lord!  And then they said, or as I prefer to say, they <u>sang</u>: *"Glory to God in the highest, and on earth peace, good will toward men."* **Luke 2:14**

What the angels were saying and what Jesus would later say; was that Jesus was coming to save the world, not condemn the world.  Jesus came to make a positive difference in the lives of people.

It was this very same Jesus who has made all the difference in my life.  He is the number one individual who has been not only my Savior, but He is my guide, my supplier, my healer, my helper, my life and eternal life. He has supplied all that I ever needed in life and did it way beyond my wildest dream. I was in no way deserving of what He has done, but He did it because He desired to do it and not because of any thing I had done.

So, to do his will is my main drive and my passion in life. There are many other passions I have in life and desires that I want to do, but His commission to me is my greatest desire. When I am actively involved in doing that and sharing Him with others, it is then that I am most happy.

I enjoy sharing **Psalm 37** with people because it speaks directly to God's involvement in the life of the believer. Check this out:

*"Trust in the Lord, and do good; dwell in the land and befriend faithfulness. Delight yourself in the Lord, and he will give you the desires of your heart. Commit your way to the Lord; trust in him, and he will act."* **Psalm 37:3-5 ESV**

This is exactly how Jesus has worked in shaping my life. I have discovered that as long as I am trusting the Lord, trusting Jesus, things just work out. I have learned also that my reaction to the events of life ought to be to do good, not retaliate in anger.

When I do good, it is an affirmation to others that my trust is in the Lord. Doing good is the way I should respond to everything in life. I should do good when it is easy and the opportunity is just right there. I should also do good when it is most difficult, during times that I have great opposition to do good. I have discovered that it is when I fret about evil deeds and dwell upon them, that I want to retaliate in defense for myself, and I become inflamed with anger and enraged with wrath. It is at those moments that I am actually only doing myself harm.

I have also come to realize that my actions in moments of conflict, though unwittingly, are shaping individuals who are influenced by me to do right or wrong. It is at these moments that I must take the next step, which is to dwell in the land, to wait out the evil deeds where I am, and then I will soon feast upon God's faithfulness as the good hand of God becomes visible. I should live my life where I am, in the situation that I find myself, and actively do that which is good, not bad.

It is the times when I have been victorious in this conflict that God gives me just what I need. He gives me the desires of my heart. It is then that I gain strength to commit my way to God, his Son Jesus, and to the leading of the Holy Spirit. It is then that I gain more trust in Him and I clearly see God act.

It is during trying times that I come to the truth and realization that my fretting and my worrying have not been my friend at all, and they are only doing me harm. Fretting just isn't worth it. The lesson is: Trust, don't worry.

God's not finished yet, because I'm not finished yet. He is still shaping my life. I have found Him to be more than sufficient for anything that may come against me. I have found Him to be the Savior that I call Him. I like the old Dallas Holm's song: *"Jesus got a hold of my life and He won't let me go!"*

What the Angel told Joseph and Mary in **Matthew 1:23** was: He is Emmanuel, God with us. Yes, Jesus is the major shaper in my life. He is my major goal in life. He is my Savior and it is at His feet that I bow.

I don't know if you know Jesus as your personal Savior or not, but may I share with you that He has made a positive impact in my life, and He definitely will make a positive impact in yours if you will trust Him.

All that I have told you is exactly what Jesus told Nicodemus in **John 3:16-21 ESV:** *"For God so loved the world, that he gave his only Son, that whoever believes in him should not perish but have eternal life. For God did not send his Son into the world to condemn the world, but in order that the world might be saved through him. Whoever believes in him is not condemned, but whoever does not believe is condemned already, because he has not believed in the name of the only Son of God. And this is the judgment that the light has come into the world, and people loved the darkness rather than the light because their works were evil. For everyone who does wicked things hates the light and does not come to the light, lest his works should be exposed. But whoever does what is true comes to the light, so that it may be clearly seen that his works have been carried out in God."*

All you need to do is to admit that you have sinned and that you are in need of a Savior. Jesus is that Savior. You need to believe that he is the saving Son of God who came to forgive you personally.

Having admitted that you have sinned, you also need to confess your sins or repent to God and ask forgiveness of those sins and The Father will forgive you because that is what Jesus came to do for you. When you have "repented" of your sins, you then begin a new life in Jesus. Repentance is merely turning around, taking a new road.

When you repent, Jesus forgives and now you are pure, clean from the sin of the past and the sin of the present and the sin of the future. Your new life has now begun, but as you live out your life you will sin. When you discover sinful deeds in your life, confess them and turn from them. Scripture tells us that God is faithful to forgive you of those sins. **1 John 1:9** *"If we confess our sins, he is faithful and just to forgive us our sins, and to cleanse us from all unrighteousness."*

Be thankful to Jesus for his forgiveness and for the gift of eternal life. Be sure to tell others about what He has done for you. Make sure you read the Bible, which is God's Word to us. Be sure to pray to Him, talk with Him, and give Him your praise. Be sure to unite with fellow believers in a Bible-believing church. Then seek to make disciples as you tell others about what Jesus has done for you in your own life.

He does make a difference, and he won't let you go.

Think about it. *Selah!*

# Day 2: Live Life To The Hilt

*"This is the day the Lord has made. We will rejoice and be glad in it."*
**Psalm 118:24 NLT**

Have you ever felt like a loser? Have you ever had a time in your life where nothing seemed to go as you thought it should go or you expected it to go? Have you ever asked God for something that you had sincerely concluded was in the will of God, and for the will of God but nothing happened? Have you ever been overlooked, passed by or been rejected for another? Have you ever felt left behind? Have you ever felt that others were purposefully scheming against you in favor of someone else? If you have, the next question is: Why is that? Why would God allow this to happen? You want to do God's will with all your heart, but every path in which you turn seems to be bogged down when others seemingly have a clear path.

I will have to admit, that there have been many times that I have experienced all those. We know that God does not show favoritism, but there are questions. Not that you are questioning God, but there are questions. There are moments of confusion.

I have come to this understanding: though I do not understand, I completely trust God with my welfare. We can relate to the lyrics of the gospel song: *"I don't know about the future but I know who holds my hand."*

Missionary Jim Elliot has said: *"Where you are, be all you can be there. Live life to the hilt."* Though I may have many questions about life and the events in life, I have no question that God has led me to where I am today and, therefore, despite the unanswered questions and confusions, I will be the light that God wants me to be and the salt that He desires me to be right where I am. Until He moves me and answers the prayer, the request, the desire that I have, I will live my life to the hilt right where I am.

Jesus told his followers: *"So don't worry about tomorrow, for tomorrow will bring its own worries. Today's trouble is enough for today."* **Matthew 6:34 NLT**

Now that is somewhat easy to say but it is a recurring battle in which I must be engaged. I seek to be like Paul when God revealed to him, though he had prayed and requested of God three times. Paul was okay with the answer: *"My grace is sufficient for you, for My strength is made perfect in weakness. Therefore most gladly I will rather boast in my infirmities, that the power of Christ may rest upon me."*
**2 Corinthians 12:9 NKJV**

If God has me where I am, I will be happy where I am and let His grace work and His strength be understood and seen in me.

One final thing, the believer must understand that God is for us. He is not against us, and if He is for us, it matters not who or what may rise up against us, **Romans 8:31.** God is for us and we are under his care. We must rest upon his faithfulness to do only what is best for us. Therefore, it is God Who has led me to where I am, and He will abundantly supply what is needed to be here. When He leads to another place, He is able to do far above anything I might expect or dream.

**Ephesians 3:20**

*"This is the day the Lord has made.  We will rejoice and be glad in it."*
**Psalm 118:24 NLT**

Think about it.  *Selah!*

## Day 3:  The Big Picture

*"I appeal to you therefore, brothers, by the mercies of God, to present your bodies as a living sacrifice, holy and acceptable to God, which is your spiritual worship. Do not be conformed to this world, but be transformed by the renewal of your mind, that by testing you may discern what is the will of God, what is good and acceptable and perfect."* **Romans 12: 1-2 ESV**

We all desire to see the big picture.  We want to know what is it that really matters in life.  How are we to view the little things in life?  Many of them are very enjoyable, pleasant and bring to us joy for the moment.  Are those little moments worthless?  No, they are not.  They are blessings in life but life consists of the little and big.   We need to look at the whole picture of life.

A key to putting together a thousand-piece puzzle is to have at hand a picture of the completed project.  If we don't have that image available our task is much more difficult.  That is the way it is in life.  The whole purpose of life is to do the will of the Father.  It is to discover that will and to be able to prove to ourselves that we are on the right path.  How that is done is by having a clear understanding of worship.  What you worship is what is important to you.  True worship, then, is living our lives in the way God desires and then worshiping Him.  We must think like God wants us to think, but we cannot think like God by using the mindset of the world.  Our minds must be in sync with God's mind. Sometimes we may refer to it as having a Biblical mindset as opposed to the world's mindset!

You may not be able to be politically correct and be

scripturally correct, or correct in God's way. God is the big picture because He created the picture. The believer's responsibility is to test things by the Holy Spirit to prove that they are indeed acceptable to God. The reason they would be acceptable to God would be the fact that they are holy thoughts and ways. If they are holy then they are not only good but also perfect.

*"I appeal to you therefore, brothers, by the mercies of God, to present your bodies as a living sacrifice, holy and acceptable to God, which is your spiritual worship. Do not be conformed to this world, but be transformed by the renewal of your mind, that by testing you may discern what is the will of God, what is good and acceptable and perfect."* **Romans 12:1 & 2 ESV**

So, what is it in your life today that you are struggling with in your search to find the big picture? Are there some questionable things that are confusing you? If they are confusing, then it is necessary that you test them to prove them to be good, holy and acceptable to God. If they are, then you are offering to God reasonable worship. If you need wisdom, ask God for wisdom and He will give it to you quickly and surely without displaying any favoritism. He is waiting with the answer. Just ask and what He says is acceptable. Seek the big picture.

Think about it. *Selah!*

### Day 4: Be Quiet

*"When the Lamb opened the seventh seal, there was silence in heaven for about half an hour."* **Revelation 8:1 ESV**

To be quiet is to have nothing to say and nothing to add. To be quiet can mean that you are in awe of a situation into which a person of great stature has entered. Fear can bring about quietness. Quietness can be the result of being in the presence of great power, transcending glory, and overcoming respect.

In Revelation everyone stood speechless for fear of what was about to be revealed. The Lamb of God in His awesome glory was about to unleash awesome wrath. The Bible tells us that for about a half hour there was nothing uttered or whispered by anyone in heaven or earth as they witnessed this event.

Peace can also bring about quietness. The peace that Jesus brought by stilling the waves and silencing the wind on that day in Galilee resulted in silence and the thought: "... Who is this that even the winds and the sea obey him?" **Mark 4:41 ESV**

Moses told the people at the Red Sea to stand still and witness the power and deliverance of their great God. God brought them deliverance and at the same time brought the Egyptians' death. **Zephaniah 3:17** tells us that God quiets us with His great love. Love can bring silence. There is nothing to fear when we are in the arms of God. If you have taken Jesus Christ as your Lord and Savior, you have this quiet peace.

Sometimes I feel that we miss a comfort from God or an encouraging word from God because we fail to just be quiet. Being quiet puts us into a situation where God can speak to us. It is interesting that we call our time before God as our quiet time. I have been told all my life that if you are talking you are not listening, and if you are not listening, you are not learning or gaining knowledge, understanding, and wisdom.

*"When the Lamb opened the seventh seal, there was silence in heaven for about half an hour."* **Revelation 8:1 ESV**

Think about it. *Selah!*

## Day 5:  Are You Hurting?

*"And let us not grow weary of doing good, for in due season we will reap, if we do not give up. So then, as we have opportunity, let us do good to everyone, especially to those who are of the household of faith."* **Galatians 6: 9-10 ESV**

Are you hurting today?  Hurt is a part of life to everyone in varying degrees.  For some of us it is a part of our daily life.

Joni Eareckson Tada, who is well acquainted with suffering on a daily basis, has written:  *"It's hard to think about heaven and how we're a blessing to others when you're hurting."*  Suffering is a daily thing for her.

Suffering is not easy because when we are hurting we need help.  When we hurt we need God to step in, and that is just what He does.  Our part is not to give up because the prize is worth the effort.  The conclusion to the matter trumps the struggle and eternity exceeds the limited time of our struggle.  Don't give up! Don't grow weary doing good, even if it hurts!

There is no struggle or any suffering or any conflict we may face that would exceed the overcoming strength that God gives His children; therefore, in the conflict, at every opportunity presented to us, do good.  It is in doing good that the power comes to overcome.  And we know that He works all things together for our good even when people do things that were carefully engineered to cause us great harm.  A good God does all things well.

*"And let us not grow weary of doing good, for in due*

*season we will reap, if we do not give up. So then, as we have opportunity, let us do good to everyone, especially to those who are of the household of faith."* **Galatians 6: 9-10 ESV**

Think about it. *Selah!*

# Day 6: Be Disgusting

*"Submit yourselves therefore to God. Resist the devil, and he will flee from you."*
**James 4:7 ESV**

Oh! That's disgusting! Something that is disgusting is offensive, sickening, repulsive and appalling. No one wants to be around a disgusting person. The disgusting person is one that you want to avoid, and his values are nothing near yours and are disgusting! The thought of a disgusting person makes your face grimace. A disgusting person is a person that you are acquainted with but not one that you want to be around.

Now, for the believer we need to seek to be disgusting to Satan. We have nothing in common with him. Satan seeks to destroy. We seek to save. He opposes God. We worship God. He is condemned by God. We are acclaimed by God. He will spend eternity in the place that was prepared especially for him and his disgusting angels, and we will spend eternity with God in a place that was especially prepared for us.

The followers of Satan have the same disgust for followers of Jesus and will do all that Satan has for them to do against us. But there is a twist here, though. We ought to desire to be disgusting to Satan and are commanded to resist him. We are commanded by God to submit to God and to do His bidding in seeking out all those who are held captive by this disgusting prince and the power of the air. We are commissioned to go into the whole world with the Good News of Salvation and make disciples of his captives. This is disgusting to Satan and he may resist our efforts; but he cannot overcome their effect.

So, be disgusting to Satan and submit to God. *"Submit yourselves therefore to God. Resist the devil, and he will flee from you."* **James 4:7 ESV**

Think about it. *Selah!*

### Day 7: Have You Ever Been Hacked?

*"When I am afraid, I put my trust in you."* **Psalm 56:3**

This morning I went to the bank to take care of my mother's bank account that was just hacked and money from her account was taken. My mother has Alzheimer's disease, and I am her fiduciary, power of attorney, and executive to manage her affairs. The reason for my visit this morning was that last night as I was checking my emails, I had an alert from her bank that her account password, email contact address, and other things had been changed. The alert asked me to contact them immediately if I was not the source of the changes. I immediately called the bank to have the account locked, and this morning I went to her local bank to check on what had been done at this point.

The bank officer was surprised in that everything was changed in such a short time and without any authorization from me. He also told me that he had to deal with acts of fraud every day and this specific tactic was new to him. To make a long story short, the bank officer was able to get to the source of the crime, and it was stopped.

How did I feel throughout all of this? I had a sinking feeling, a fear of the unknown, and a helpless feeling in wondering if I had done all that was needed to be done. At this point I needed to trust my banking officer. My security was in him and his knowledge of what needed to be done.

People bring fear and events cause fears to arise. Personal ineptness, lack of ability, and limited knowledge are the source of many of the fears in our lives. What conquers fear is power. God is all-powerful, so if God is the bank in Whom I have put my trust, then I need to trust Him, His power and the promise of care.

The Psalmist David writes: *"When I am afraid, I put my trust in you"* **Psalm 56:3 ESV.** David acknowledges that he has had times of fear and apparently was in a moment of fear at the time he wrote this Psalm and it was his confidence in God that turned his fear to peace through trust. Paul writes: "If God is for us, who can be against us?" **Romans 8:31** The answer is nothing and no one.

Fear will come into our lives from time to time. When it does, remember that for the duration of the fear, we must trust God for He is faithful.

Think about it. *Selah!*

# Day 8: Disciplined

*"For the moment all discipline seems painful rather than pleasant, but later it yields the peaceful fruit of righteousness to those who have been trained by it."*
**Hebrews 12:11 ESV**

Discipline is not punishment.  It is training which corrects error, molds to truth, and strengthens for resilience and durability.  It moves one toward perfection.  Some may discipline with anger and in doing so that discipline is uncomfortable and painful. After it is endured, however, it produces pride, confidence, stability and peace.  People who are proficient in anything have endured a long road of discipline and have experienced many moments where the thought of quitting has tempted them, but they endured.  They disciplined themselves and the discipline made them shine.  Discipline shows off its product, which is excellence.  It makes us exceed our expectations and go well beyond the reach of the undisciplined.  Others envy a disciplined person.  He is respected, inspirational, and a model or pattern for others to follow.

We read in **2 Timothy 3:16** that all of Scripture is inspired by God.  God is the measuring stick and Scripture is His thought and word. God is complete. He is perfection.  He is total wisdom and knowledge.  Therefore, we find Scripture to be useful because we are incomplete, imperfect, unlearned, and at times clueless in our need of correction or alignment to the pattern of perfection. Scripture brings attention to error. Scripture is a discipline to follow, and when we apply the Scriptures to our lives, we become more disciplined and ready for the struggles of life.

We then will become admired by others, sought out, singled out, and held in high esteem by others. We also will be unfairly complained against, attacked, ridiculed, persecuted, and falsely accused by others because of the achievements we have reached. The fruit of the disciplined life threatens the life of false pride.

So seek that which is good and perfect. Seek to know and do the will of God for your life, and that will take discipline. It is not a bad thing, but it is a hard thing.

*"For the moment all discipline seems painful rather than pleasant, but later it yields the peaceful fruit of righteousness to those who have been trained by it."* **Hebrews 12:11 ESV**

Think about it. *Selah!*

### Day 9:  Dog Bite

*"For we do not wrestle against flesh and blood, but against the rulers, against the authorities, against the cosmic powers over this present darkness, against the spiritual forces of evil in the heavenly places."* **Ephesians 6:12 ESV**

If you and some of your friends were out for a walk and were all attacked by a rabid dog, it would be tragic. Some may have died from the attack and others may have recovered, but all would be traumatized by the episode.  The neighborhood would certainly be up in arms.  What would be the concern and where would the battle be here?  Is it with the dogs?  What about their teeth?  Could it be their saliva?  No, the battle is against the rabies virus, and there is an antiviral vaccine that can conquer it.  The vaccine attacks the virus and renders it powerless.

The battle and war that we face is not what is seen.  It is the powerful unseen that causes suffering, death, and trauma.  Paul writes in **Ephesians 6:12** *"For we do not wrestle against flesh and blood, but against the rulers, against the authorities, against the cosmic powers over this present darkness, against the spiritual forces of evil in the heavenly places."* **ESV**

We see this misdirection against violence everywhere today.  It is not the gun, the bomb, or the political party. It is the sin that so easily overtakes us.  It is the great power that only God is able to conquer.  We must see the real battle and actual source of the evil and stand against it.  It is not the person; it is the unseen power that has attacked the person and caused that person to do what is wrong and evil. That same truth can be understood with the violence that we see in our world today. Satan and his angels have infected humanity and our world. God did not make it that way. Satan did. It is hard not to focus on and take vengeance upon the flesh and blood that we see involved in the committing of sin.

Again, the battle is not against others. It is against principalities and powers. So, here is the challenge: Put on the whole armor, the vaccine that God has given us for the battle, and stand. Don't look at others. They are not the problem. Remember that once we were like them before we were saved. *"And you were dead in the trespasses and sins in which you once walked, following the course of this world, following the prince of the power of the air, the spirit that is now at work in the sons of disobedience--among whom we all once lived in the passions of our flesh, carrying out the desires of the body and the mind, and were by nature children of wrath, like the rest of mankind."* **Ephesians 2:1-3 ESV**

Think about it. *Selah!*

## Day 10:  By Invitation Only

*"Worry weighs a person down; an encouraging word cheers a person up".*
**Proverbs 12:25 NLT**

What are the chances of the children of the wealthiest person in the world not having enough food for tomorrow, not having sufficient clothing for the winter, or wondering where they would live?  We could say with great certainty that there would be nothing to be concerned about here and any anxiety fostered by the children would be unfounded.

In **Matthew 6:25-34** Jesus assures his followers that any concern for the necessities of life is unfounded and that if they would just consider how the Father takes care of creation, then their anxieties, worries, and concerns would vanish.  If we are doing what we are supposed to do, God will take care of the rest.

Solomon writes in **Proverbs 12:25** that worry and anxiety are unnecessary weights that are harmful, burdensome, and hindrances in our life.  If they are unnecessary, then they are uninvited.  So, I could say that if they exist in our lives, we have invited them in and have given them a false credibility.  If we do not invite them in, they cannot be part of our lives.

One more thing, we can bring worry and anxiety into the lives of others, or we can be an encouragement and bring life and good cheer.  Are people happy to see you, or are you a weight, a burden, and a hindrance to their lives?

*"Worry weighs a person down; an encouraging word cheers a person up".* **Proverbs 12:25 ESV**

Think about it. *Selah!*

## Day 11: What Do You See?

*"How can you say to your brother, 'Brother, let me take out the speck that is in your eye.' when you yourself do not see the log that is in your own eye?"* **Luke 6:42 ESV**

Have you ever tried to edit your own writing? I do but I always overlook many errors. But if I ask someone else to read over the paper, they are quick to see what I have overlooked. The same is true in our daily lives. We are quick to see the errors in others' lives and seemingly blind to our own. We need others in our lives to help us mature as a person, a Christian, and a follower of Jesus Christ; yet, we resist the correction. We complain when others expose our faults, feeling them to be too harsh. We meet the obvious changes that need to be made with retaliation and destructive criticism.

Remember, you cannot improve unless you remove that which needs the improvement, that which is holding you back. Have you heard this phrase used in advertisement: "New and Improved"? Well, that means that something was missing, lacking or needed to make that product more effective. The same is true in our lives, and we must always be improving and moving to a newer and more improved life in Christ.

Remember, we are not perfect and never will be, but Christ Jesus is perfect. So, what I am saying is, at least consider your error which is seen by others and do not be so quick to look at the error of others. If you do see an error in someone else's life, seek to be a help, a friend, and a fellow laborer in the ministry. Remember to remove what is obvious in your own life before you attempt to point out the inconspicuous to your friend.

*"How can you say to your brother, 'Brother, let me take out the speck that is in your eye.' when you yourself do not see the log that is in your own eye?"* **Luke 6:42 ESV**

Think about it. *Selah!*

# Day 12: Have A Good Day!

*"It is good to give thanks to the Lord, to sing praises to your name, O Most High; to declare your steadfast love in the morning, and your faithfulness by night,"*
**Psalm 92:1-2 ESV**

As we leave the company of others after having conversation with them, it is almost customary to say, "Have a nice day." In saying this, we are hoping they will experience all the good that God has for them that day. It means we hope that those individuals with whom we have enjoyed conversing and having a pleasant experience with will in turn experience the same pleasantry the rest of the day because they have added to our lives for the good.

The Psalmist here points out that a day that is begun with conversation with God and focuses upon His great name and His faithful, steadfast love displayed to us brings joy. That conversation is an encouragement to us for the rest of the day. That appointment at the beginning of the day brings joy throughout the day.

At the conclusion of our day as we meet once again with our faithful and loving God, we recount and affirm again his faithfulness and love experienced throughout our day, and it gives us peace for the night. As we focus upon God at the start of the day we are encouraged to endure. We are equipped to share with others the great God in our lives. We have fresh ammunition to use in the battle of the day.; so, have that special quiet time in the morning with your God and return at night to acknowledge His faithfulness. Thank Him for the good day. Yes, we did have a good day.

*"It is good to give thanks to the Lord, to sing praises to your name, O Most High; to declare your steadfast love in the morning, and your faithfulness by night,"* **Psalm 92:1-2 ESV**

Think about it. *Selah!*

## Day 13: Surpassing Understanding

*"Do not be anxious about anything, but in everything by prayer and supplication with thanksgiving let your requests be made known to God. And the peace of God, which surpasses all understanding, will guard your hearts and your minds in Christ Jesus."* **Philippians 4:6-7 ESV**

*"Beyond all understanding,"* what is that? That means that you have encountered something in your life that has exceeded your personal capacity to fully understand. You have come across something that cannot be believed based upon the understanding and knowledge that you have at the moment. It defies all that is within you, and it goes against all that you have experienced. We judge things by what we know. You accept things according to the understanding that you have accumulated, and this just exceeds your ability to comprehend.

This peace is such an experience. God's peace in itself gives evidence of the existence of God for it is something that only God can give. God's peace is not earned. It is given. This peace cannot be bought, sold or hoarded. It is a blessing from God alone. Suffering summons it, tragedy reveals it, and calamity is bathed with it. God saturates all of these circumstances in His all-sufficient grace in order for us to endure them.

Because this peace is beyond our understanding does not affect its truth. Because it seems to be unreasonable does not diminish its power. Because it is too good to be true does not prevent it. Because you just cannot believe it does not contradict it. The only response to it is thanksgiving. This peace of God beckons our praise toward God, gives glory to God, and gives us a reason for our worship of God.

The song "What a Friend We Have in Jesus" captures some of these moments of peace. This peace is found in Jesus bearing our sins and grief. Peace is found in triumph over discouragement, as a refuge in overloaded lives, in times of weakness, and in the listening ear of Jesus when we have been forgotten, rejected, and lied about. Throughout all of life's struggles stands God's peace, unbelievable yet undeniable, beyond our understanding but validated by God's faithfulness and presence.

*"Do not be anxious about anything, but in everything by prayer and supplication with thanksgiving let your requests be made known to God. And the peace of God, which surpasses all understanding, will guard your hearts and your minds in Christ Jesus."* **Philippians 4:6-7 ESV**

Think about it. *Selah*

# Day 14:  An Amazing God

*"And they sing the song of Moses, the servant of God, and the song of the Lamb, saying,*
*Great and amazing are your deeds,*
*O Lord God the Almighty!*
*Just and true are your ways,*
*O King of the nations!"* **Revelation 15:3 ESV**

That is amazing!  Amazing means astonishment, being surprised, or stunned. It is breath taking and a wonder. All these things are what God is.  God is astonishing.  He is unbelievable.  He defies and goes beyond human understanding. We are stunned by his deeds, actions, and character.   To think of Him brings about a sense of wonder, and stunning, breath-taking sights.   God is amazing to our mind!

We cannot understand God because He is.  He had no beginning.   When Moses asked God His name at the burning bush, God's response was: "I Am," and He is.  I like how A. W. Tozer defined God: *"God knows all things perfectly. He knows no thing better than any other thing, but all things equally well.  He never discovers anything. He is never surprised, never amazed.  He never wonders about anything nor (except when drawing men out for their own good) does he seek information or ask questions. God is self-existent and self-contained and knows what no creature can ever know--HIMSELF, perfectly."*

Yes, God is amazing!  There is never anything about you that God did not always know.  You cannot surprise God by your actions, thoughts or deeds.  Before the foundation of this world, God had already written down in His book the day you would be born, the duration of your life and every thought, intent, and event in your life. He knew if you would accept His offer of salvation or not and did not interfere in your decision-making. Though you are a free moral agent, He knows your every move. **Psalm 139:16**

If you decide to reject Him, He still is loving to you and patient with you. If you decide to receive Him as your Lord and Savior, He knows all your failures and moments of defeat. God knows the sin that so easily defeats you, and He never grows tired of your request for forgiveness. You are His child, His sheep, and He knows you and you know Him, **John 10:2-4; 1 Corinthians 2:11.** Yes, God is amazing!

*"And they sing the song of Moses, the servant of God, and the song of the Lamb, saying,*
> *Great and amazing are your deeds,*
> *O Lord God the Almighty!*
> *Just and true are your ways,*
> *O King of the nations!"* **Revelation 15:3 ESV**

Think about it. *Selah!*
## Day 15: "The Great Courtesy Of God"

*"Beloved, let us love one another, for love is from God, and whoever loves has been born of God and knows God. Anyone who does not love does not know God, because God is love."* **1 John 4:7-8 ESV**

The Scottish scholar, James Mofatt, wrote: "Jesus prohibits any restriction of love and pity to those who are unkind to ourselves." Love of God and others cannot be separated, and if we love then we also have a holy pity upon others. Francis of Assisi calls this display of love and concern for all as "The Great Courtesy of God". God is kind to all and it is His great kindness and love that brings men to conviction and salvation. It is a courtesy of God. A courtesy is a politeness shown to others. It is not a requirement. It is freely and gladly given to another and given with love and respect. God is just but He also is love and His love is displayed by his patience and pity for us. **2 Peter 3:9 NLT** says, "*. . . he is being patient for your sake.*" Love is the very basic makeup of God and the followers of God must be like Him and display His characteristics in their daily lives.

Since this is the foundational makeup of God, then we too must display that love. We must reflect it to those who despitefully use us, to those who oppose us, and to all those outside the love of God. But it does not end there. We must love one another and by this love, others will know that we are followers of Christ. **1 John 3:18-19 NLT says,** *"Dear children, let's not merely say that we love each other; let us show the truth by our actions. Our actions will show that we belong to the truth, so we will be confident when we stand before God."*

Love is a courtesy that we owe to all. It is just a courtesy. *"Beloved, let us love one another, for love is from God, and whoever loves has been born of God and knows God. Anyone who does not love does not know God, because God is love."* **1 John 4:7-8 ESV**

Think about it. *Selah!*

## Day 16: Think On These Things

*"Finally, brothers, whatever is true, whatever is honorable, whatever is just, whatever is pure, whatever is lovely, whatever is commendable, if there is any excellence, if there is anything worthy of praise, think about these things."* **Philippians 4:8 ESV**

How do you deal with controversy? What is your mindset in disagreements? Can you relate to those who may be hateful to you? How do you react to those who treat you with disdain and spite? I will have to admit that I fall woefully short in each of these areas and have to battle daily to maintain the mind of Christ.

I am sure you have heard the saying, *"I guess we must agree to disagree."* On that we all can agree. All do not always understand the truth. Being misunderstood is a frequently occurring event in everyone's life as well; therefore, disagreement is apt to appear. But it is how we deal with controversy and disagreement that shapes our relationships with one another. What goes through our minds in controversy and disagreement determines the outcome and future relationships in our lives. Paul tells us in **Philippians 4:8** to think about honorable and praiseworthy things. There were two ladies in the church of Philippi who were involved in such a battle, Euodia and Syntyche. They worked together in the church, they loved the same Lord, the same God, but a disagreement surfaced and a battle ensued. The answer was for the church members to help change how these two ladies were thinking. Paul was asking each member in that church to not enter into the disagreement and controversy but to defuse it by injecting moments of truth and thoughts of honorable things, just things, pure things, lovely things, and things that are commendable and excellent which would bring about the mindset of praise to God.

*"Finally, brothers, whatever is true, whatever is honorable, whatever is just, whatever is pure, whatever is lovely, whatever is commendable, if there is any excellence, if there is anything worthy of praise, think about these things."* **Philippians 4:8 ESV**

Think about it. *Selah!*

## Day 17: Let The Redeemed Of The Lord Say So

*"Oh give thanks to the Lord, for he is good, for his steadfast love endures forever! Let the redeemed of the Lord say so, whom he has redeemed from trouble."*
**Psalm 107: 1-2 ESV**

Have you ever been in trouble?  Ridiculous question isn't it?  Trouble is a reoccurring event of life and getting free from trouble is a major part of the event.  When the troubling event is solved and we have been relieved of the burden and the burden has been lifted, we feel like shouting.

Did you know that is exactly what God has done for us through Jesus Christ?  He took our trouble, the sin that daily brought conviction and so easily enslaved us, and He destroyed it.  He blotted it out from the books of our sins, writing "paid in full," and transferred our name to the ***Book of Life***.  At the moment of our conversion we became a whole new creation, a new person with a new future.  We have been redeemed! That is something to shout about!!  *"Oh give thanks to the Lord, for he is good, for his steadfast love endures forever! Let the redeemed of the Lord say so, whom he has redeemed from trouble."*
**Psalm 107:1-2 ESV**

So shout to the Lord and give thanks!  This is a time for glad tidings, for God has been faithful and He will remain faithful, though we might not.  What a great love is His steadfast, enduring, and eternal love for us!

I feel like telling someone, don't you?

Think about it.  *Selah!*

## Day 18:  Why Would God Love Me?

*"Whoever confesses that Jesus is the Son of God, God abides in him, and he in God.  So we have come to know and to believe the love that God has for us.  God is love, and whoever abides in love abides in God, and God abides in him."* **1 John 4:15-16 ESV**

To understand that God is pure and has no fault, no stain or imperfection of any kind, and cannot sin, causes one to wonder: *Why would such a God love me?*

The answer is He desires to love you because He chooses to love you.  He wants to love because He is love, real and pure love.  God loves you because He sees you to be in need of love, devoid of love, empty and without help.  He sees us in need of His love and He has displayed it through His Son, Jesus.  Jesus proves that God loves you because you need Him and He desires to love you.

When we place our acts of love next to His pure love it is obvious that there is nothing that is lovable about us. You might think your white socks are clean but when you place them beside an unstained sock, the stains are clearly visible even to our eye.

Back to the question, why would God love me?  It is because He chooses to love us, and we love Him because He first loved us.  Our love is in response to His love.  It is conditional to His unconditional love.  **Romans 5:8 & Ephesians 2:4**

You cannot figure out God's love for it is divine, and we are human. We cannot figure it out because He is the creator and we are His creation.  Therefore, we must accept God's love, believe God's love, trust God's love, and then enjoy God's love. He loved us first and we then love Him. **1 John 4:19**

John tells us to love each other with that same love that Jesus loved his Father, and it is unique to God. *"Beloved, let us love one another, for love is from God, and whoever loves has been born of God and knows God"* **1 John 4:7 ESV.** *"By this all people will know that you are my disciples, if you have love for one another."* **John 13:35 ESV**

*"Whoever confesses that Jesus is the Son of God, God abides in him, and he in God. So we have come to know and to believe the love that God has for us. God is love, and whoever abides in love abides in God, and God abides in him."* **1 John 4:15-16 ESV**

Yep! God loves you because he wants to love you.

Think about it. *Selah!*

## Day 19: It Doesn't Take A Theologian To Explain The Good News

*"For God so loved the world, that he gave his only Son, that whoever believes in him should not perish but have eternal life. For God did not send his Son into the world to condemn that world, but in order that the world might be saved through him."*
**John 3: 16-17 ESV**

The Good News is that Jesus Christ came into the world to save sinners, the great sinners, and all others as well. God is not looking for people who are good in the eyes of the world but those who are guilty and understand that they are. The Good News is offered to the condemned of this world and that includes the whole world.

God does not ask for applications, resumes, or letters of recommendation. The Good News is offered to all, open to all, free to all, and extended to all without exception. He alone is the judge. He alone holds the offer. The Holy Spirit is the drawer, the convicter, the teacher, and the restrainer. The responsibility of His followers is to be the bearer of the Good News. All we are to do is to carry it. Never get into the habit of judging the salvation of others. God is the judge, not you.

We are witnesses of God's kindness, love, mercy and grace, and this leads others to repentance. *"Or do you presume on the riches of his kindness and forbearance and patience, not knowing that God's kindness is meant to lead you to repentance?"* **Romans 2:4 ESV**

So carry the Good News, tell others the Good News, and let God work in their lives. It's simple. You don't need to be a theologian. *"For God so loved the world, that he gave his only Son, that whoever believes in him should not perish but have eternal life. For God did not send his Son into the world to condemn that world, but in order that the world might be saved through him."* **John 3: 16-17 ESV**

Think about it. *Selah!*

# Day 20: The Work Of A Father

*"See what kind of love the Father has given to us, that we should be called children of God; and so we are. The reason why the world does not know us is that it did not know him. Beloved, we are God's children now, and what we will be has not yet appeared; but we know that when he appears we shall be like him, because we shall see him as he is."* **1 John 3:1 & 2 ESV**

To see you as you are, to see the real you is to be able to see the genuine you, the undisputable you. This is what our family needs to see, to see us as we are. A father who genuinely loves his family is followed, loved, and patterned after. As we try to be like Jesus and the Father, our children and grandchildren will do the same. A godly father should be seen caring for his wife, and his wife will care for him in return. But that fatherly love does not end there. It extends to our extended family, our friends, and their friends. This is a good example to be followed.

What a godly father does:
- He asks God for wisdom and guidance and trusts Him to provide as He promised.
- He acknowledges God exceeding his efforts with God's grace.
- He works with his faithful wife in the shaping of his children to be champions for Christ.
- He recognizes faithful patterns in other faithful fathers.
- He does not talk negatively about others around his children. Children love their father and hate those who despitefully use him.
- He includes his children in ministry events.

- He makes plans to position his children around other Christ-minded children.
- He shares struggles with his children and points out God's hand in the struggle.
- He praises his wife openly and genuinely.

Desire and make it your aim to be a Godly father. Follow the lead of God our Father.

*"Beloved, we are God's children now, and what we will be has not yet appeared; but we know that when he appears we shall be like him, because we shall see him as he is."* **1 John 3:2 ESV**

Think about it. *Selah!*

# Day 21:  Falling Short

*". . . for all have sinned and fall short of the glory of God."* **Romans 3:23 ESV**

Have you ever fallen short of a goal?  Do you know what it is like to miss the mark that you have set for yourself or that someone else may have set for you?  Has your banking account ever been overdrawn because of your failure to keep sufficient records?

Did you know that you are unable by yourself to meet the demands of God?  Did you know that you cannot be good enough for heaven on your own? Did you know that God is not looking for good people because there are no good people on this earth?  Jesus tells us that there is none good, no not one. **Mark 10:18 & Romans 3:10**

Any attempt we make to get to heaven on our own will only fall woefully short and miss the mark set by God. You see, we are helpless on our own.  Our account has been hacked, and there are insufficient funds available to pay the debt that we owe.  Fortunately, we have a donor, a redeemer who has the funds needed and wants to place our name on His bank of heaven.  Jesus does not fall short.  He fulfilled the plan.  He has completed the requirements and written: "It is finished," **John 19:30 ESV.**  All things have been made new and it is done, **Revelation 21:6.**

Though we fall short from God's glory, Jesus is the glory of the Father and the fulfillment of His plan.  God is not looking for good people.  He is looking for dead people who need eternal life.  What about you? Have you fallen short of the mark?  Have you admitted that you are helpless on your own and need a Savior, a Redeemer? Jesus is the one and we can trust Him.

*"...for all have sinned and fall short of the glory of God."*
**Romans 3:23 ESV**

Think about it. *Selah!*

## Day 22:  Security Has Been Compromised!

*"Be sober-minded; be watchful.  Your adversary the devil prowls around like a roaring lion, seeking someone to devour."* **1 Peter 5:8 ESV**

I received a notice from my bank inquiring about some suspicious activity that had taken place.  The notice proved to be true and the bottom line was that someone had made changes to that account and taken funds from it.  Fortunately, I caught it before the hacker could complete the desired evil deeds.  I am thankful for the watchful eye of my bank security system caring for the unsuspecting me.

It is sad to know that there are others prowling around in our world seeking out unsuspecting individuals that they might pounce upon for their own personal pleasure.  It takes a lot of work to do those evil deeds.  It takes persistence, ambition, sacrifice and dedication.  This sounds like traits we teach our children in becoming an asset to God and to faithfully work in his assignments to us and to society in general.  We want our children to be successful.  Satan also wants his followers to be successful in doing his evil deeds.  Therefore, we need to be watchful and sober, looking all around for the unexpected because Satan is crafty, stealthy, cunning, and is empowering those under his control to do the same deceitful things.

*"Be sober-minded; be watchful.  Your adversary the devil prowls around like a roaring lion, seeking someone to devour."* **1 Peter 5:8 ESV**

Don't use Satan's methods; use God's methods of love, joy, peace, gentleness, goodness, kindness, faithfulness and self-control to defeat the cunning craftiness of Satan, **Galatians 5:22**.

Think about it. *Selah!*

## Day 23: Do Believers Fail?

*"For we must all appear before the judgment seat of Christ, so that each one may receive what is due for what he has done in the body, whether good or evil"*
**2 Corinthians 5:10 ESV**

Judgment means a decision must be made about the rightness or wrongness of something.  If something is wrong then there was a failure to reach a goal or a failure to fulfill an assignment.  A believer can fail but failure was not due to insufficient power or supply. It was due to the failure of the one assigned.

Written in the fly leaf of one of the books my Dad had on prayer, he wrote these words:  *"If we have the Father, the power of the Holy Spirit, and the leadership of Jesus, what are we to say if we lose the battle?"* We have nothing to say.  If the battle is lost, it is because we failed in some way.

You see, we can do all things through Christ Jesus our Lord, **Philippians 4:13**.  We have been supplied with all that we need for our assignment and more, **Philippians 4:19.**  God is faithful at all times and cannot be anything but faithful.  The caution is that we must be diligent in the work or we may fail.  If we begin to do it in our strength we get weak.

Paul tells the Ephesian believers that life is worth little unless we use it to do the assignment that God has given us and that assignment is to tell others about the Good News of God's great kindness and love for them, **Acts 20:24.**

There will be a judgment of the deeds of the believers and that will be at the Judgment Seat of Christ. We will not be judged at this time for our eternal life or for our entrance into heaven. That will be done at the Great White Throne Judgment for the unbeliever, **Revelation 20:11-15.** The believer will be judged for his or her work done on earth at the Judgment Seat of Christ where all the things done for the cause of Christ while on the earth will be judged as to their goodness or evil. Rewards will be given and rewards will be taken away.

*"For we must all appear before the judgment seat of Christ, so that each one may receive what is due for what he has done in the body, whether good or evil"*
**2 Corinthians 5:10 ESV**

The believer can fail, but he cannot lose his eternal home in heaven. Jesus secured it.

Think about it. *Selah!*

## Day 24: Opportunities: *For Such A Time As This*

*"For if you keep silent at this time, relief and deliverance will rise for the Jews from another place, but you and your father's house will perish. And who knows whether you have not come to the kingdom for such a time as this?"*
**Esther 4:14 ESV**

In Shakespeare's *Julius Caesar,* he writes:

> *"There is a tide in the affairs of men,*
> *Which, taken at the flood, leads on to fortune,*
> *Omitted, all the voyages of their life*
> *Is bound in shallows and in miseries."*

Everyone else might say, "Opportunity knocks but once." That's not too flowery, but it says what it says. Others have said, "Opportunity knocks but once but misfortune leans on the doorbell."

Perhaps I could say, be ready for opportunity knocks but once. It is true in life, and it is especially true in the ministry and in service to God. When God opens doors, He lets us make the decision. Once the decision is made, that is the way it will be with us.

It was the rich young ruler who wanted to be used by Jesus. He was rich, he was young, and he was a ruler in the land at a young age. But when Jesus opened the door of opportunity before him, he was unwilling to step through the door. The opportunity passed him by because he was unwilling to make the sacrifice that was necessary to be part of the offered opportunity. We know that Jesus loved him and wanted to use him, but the young man was not willing. His accomplishments stood in his way. I often wonder what happened to that young man.

The call of God requires obedience and watchfulness at all times for the call. When we obey the call of God, He then makes all the provisions, provides all the planning, overcomes every obstacle, and is the total source of strength. Everything stands upon our obedience, total obedience.

When we obey, it is then that marvelous things begin to happen, doors swing open, and we see people saved and lives changed. God can do exceeding abundantly above all that we might have the faith to ask or even think. As Eugene Peterson puts it, " *. . . in your wildest dreams!*" **Ephesians 3:20 MSG.**

Here is the fear factor: If we fail to act, God's will is going to be done. If we don't act, God will use someone else to fulfill His will, but our families and we will not receive the blessing and will suffer the consequences that may arrive from our lack of faith.

That is what Mordecai was telling his niece, Queen Esther. God could use her now, but if she hesitated, relief would come because God had a plan. The question to her was: Was she willing to be used in that plan?

So the offer is open to you: *Who knows but that God has placed you into this nation, these United States of America, ". . . for such a time as this?"* **Esther 4:14b ESV**

Think about it. *Selah!*

### Day 25: Conclusion: *What Have You Been Given?*

*"Everyone to whom much was given, of him much will be required, and from him to who they entrusted much, they will demand the more."* **Luke 12:48 ESV**

When Jesus was walking the dusty roads of Israel, why was it that the very people who should have been the most receptive to the message of Jesus (*"Except you repent of your sins, you will all perish"*) were the most resistant to His message? I mean, weren't the priests and educators expecting the Messiah? Certainly, they knew what was written in the Scriptures and proclaimed all through them. Surely they should have understood and seen what was happening before them. But they didn't see or understand. Why couldn't they see *Who* it was before them?

Jesus did not hide his message. He did not deny *Who* He was at any time. The first thing that is recorded about Jesus, apart from being with parents, was that He was found in the temple explaining Scripture to the priests, lawyers, scribes and teachers. The Bible says that they were astonished at His understanding and His ability to explain the meaning and intent of Scripture.

When Joseph and Mary found Him and inquired of Him as to why he did not stay with the group, He answered with a question: *"Did you not know that I must be about my Father's business?"* **Luke 2:49 NKJV.** This was, after all, the very reason that He came; His very purpose that was informed to Joseph and Mary by the angel, and the business that the Father had planned for His Son all along. Joseph and Mary had to press the reset button, but the leaders were humiliated and pressed the "get rid of the boy" button.

The leaders could not see because their eyes were darkened by their desires for personal recognition and praise. Their desires were not for the glory of God. Their intentions were far from the intentions of God and far from the purpose that they were given by God. They could not see God although He stood before them. They could not see Him because they were far from God. They did not even know God though they had studied all their lives about Him. There was no excuse for them.

God expected much more from them because they had been given much and been given much more than the others. He expected more from them than the publicans, sinners, tax collectors, drunkards, and the like. Now they were in great danger because their punishment would be much, much more grievous than others. Jesus spent more of his time around these outcasts. *"Everyone to whom much was given, of him much will be required, and from him to who they entrusted much, they will demand the more."* **Luke 12:48 ESV**

Because God has done great things for my family and me, much more is expected from us. And God will require even greater things in the future. I am not judged by the standards of others, and I cannot be content with meeting the standards of others. The standard that God has given my family and me is much higher. To whom much is given, much more is required. That is an awesome responsibility and one in which I want to be found faithful.

What about you? What about your church? Has God done marvelous things through you and your church? If so, He requires much, much more of you and your church. You must not slow down. You must press on.

Do not allow Satan to cause you to be satisfied with the way things are and to be proud of what God has done through you. God requires much more of you. Press on, reach toward the prize, strip off the things that hinder you, and run the race with fervency. God chose this race for you. Run well. Don't look at the race of others. Run your race!

Think about it. *Selah!*

### Day 26:  Thoughts: What Do You Think?

*"O Lord, the God of Abraham, Isaac, and Israel, our fathers, keep forever such purposes and thoughts in the hearts of your people, and direct their hearts toward you."*
**1 Chronicles 29:18 ESV**

*"The thoughts of the righteous are just; the counsels of the wicked are deceitful."*
**Proverbs 12:5 ESV**

*"For I know the plans I have for you, declares the Lord, plans for welfare and not for evil, to give you a future and a hope."* **Jeremiah 29:11 ESV**

*"Finally, brothers, whatever is true, whatever is honorable, whatever is just, whatever is pure, whatever is lovely, whatever is commendable, if there is any excellence, if there is anything worthy of praise, think about these things."* **Philippians 4:8 ESV**

*"For out of the abundance of the heart the mouth speaks."* **Matthew 12:34 ESV**

It is said, *"An idle mind, is the devil's workshop."*  And that is true.  If you are doing nothing, Satan is doing something; therefore, do something, be involved, take action.  While you are doing, look for those things that are true, honorable, just, pure, lovely commendable, excellent, and praise worthy.  Aggressively and purposefully think on these types of things, **Philippians 4:8-9.**  Let's think about some good things.

Think about it.  *Selah!*

## Day 27:  Let All The Earth Rejoice And Sing Praises!

*"Beside them the birds of the heavens dwell; they sing among the branches."*
**Psalm 104:12 ESV**

I didn't sleep much last night, so I got up earlier than normal.  I got ready and decided to go to *Starbucks* to get a cup of coffee.  The sun wasn't quite up as I got into my car, and there was what I would describe as a pleasant chill on this spring morning just before sunrise.  By the time I arrived at *Starbucks* and got out of the car, I heard the most cheerful bird chirping with all that was within him.

The exuberance of that little bird invited me to join in, as he *"sang among the branches"* where he was perched. He was doing what he was created to do, sing of the glory of the Lord, the Creator of heaven and earth.  *"The heavens declare the glory of God, and the sky above proclaims his handiwork."* **Psalm 19:1 ESV**

The smile that began to burst upon my face took its lead from the rising sun, it began to beam and lighten up my side of the earth.  By the time I left *Starbucks,* the sun had filled the darkness with its brilliant light.  The sun too, was doing what it was created to do and brought with it warmth to this beautiful morning.  *"The heavens declare the glory of God, and the sky above proclaims his handiwork.  Day to day pours out speech, and night to night reveals knowledge. There is no speech, nor are there words, whose voice is not heard. Their voice goes out through all the earth, and their words to the end of the world.  In them he has set a tent for the sun, which comes out like a bridegroom leaving his chamber, and, like a strong man, runs its course with joy. Its rising is from the end of the heavens, and its circuit to the end of them, and there is nothing hidden from its heat."* **Psalm 19:1-6 ESV**

My night of tossing was turned to thoughts of my great God and joy flooded my mind just by creation doing what it was created to do. I began to think, why is it that the crown of God's creation, mankind, does not do what it was created to do? Why are we not engaged in glorifying our Creator and magnifying His name daily in worship? The reason for the trouble in this troubled world is that mankind is troubled by sin. He cannot bring glory to God until he turns his eyes off the trouble and onto his Creator and begins to do what he was created to do, which is, worship God. When we begin to worship, the darkness of the day will all seem to vanish by the rising of God's Son in our lives.

Now, how about you? Why not decide today to forget about those troubles in your life, remember why you were created, and start doing what you were created to do. I am quite certain that when you do, all those troubles will leave and will be replaced with the joy of the Creator, our Lord. As in the lyrics of the hymn, "Turn Your Eyes Upon Jesus" written by Helen Lemmel, when we *"look full in His wonderful face, . . . the things of earth will grow strangely dim, in the light of His glory and grace."* It will invade our darkness and turn it to day.

*"Let the words of my mouth and the meditation of my heart be acceptable in your sight, O Lord, my rock and my redeemer."* **Psalm 19:14 ESV**

Think about it. *Selah!*

### Day 28: Wait A Minute!

*"And though the Lord give you the bread of adversity and the water of affliction, yet your Teacher will not hide himself anymore, but your eyes shall see your Teacher. And your ears shall hear a word behind you, saying, 'This is the way, walk in it,' when you turn to the right or when you turn to the left."* **Isaiah 30:20-21 ESV**

I do not like to wait. I don't want to slow down in anyway. I don't like traffic, I don't like red lights, I don't like lines, I don't like Disney Land, I don't do Black Friday, not even Gray Thursday. I have no desire to even go shopping. Shopping means that you are not sure what you are looking for. The reason I go to a store is to buy a specific thing, and I expect the store to have what I want. I don't want to have a rain check because that means I have to wait. My favorite phrase in the Bible is *"Go ye therefore, . . ."* **Matthew 28:19.**

When things aren't right or something goes wrong in my day, I respond with the worst phrase I can think of: "WAIT A MINUTE!" That means I'm really upset.

The sad truth is, I need to get over it. Waiting is a real part of life. Have you ever noticed how often the word wait is used in following the Lord? Just the word "follow" means you don't know where you are going. It means I am not leading. It means that I am waiting on the Leader to make the move. I wait for Him to move and when He does move, I must follow. I must go without hesitation. (I like that part.) The last thing Jesus told His disciples was to stay and wait. **Acts 1:4** (There is a learning curve for me.)

You may think that you don't have that problem, but I think I would be safe in saying that when you pray, you don't want to wait for an answer. You are looking for an answer right now or at least by the end of the day.

We don't want to have to experience afflictions or have adversity or be involved in conflict in any way because that makes us wait. We don't like training because we have to wait before we actually get in the game. Choirs and instrumental groups don't like rehearsal because we have to wait for others to get their part after we get ours. But waiting is what makes us strong. Waiting brings knowledge, understanding, and wisdom.

The truth is we are going to have problems in our lives and we need to learn to wait through those problems. *"Blessed is the man who remains steadfast under trial, for when he has stood the test he will receive the crown of life, which God has promised to those who love him."* **James 1:12 ESV**

Actually, I am not quite as bad as I have portrayed myself, but I do have a tendency to hurry and not wait. If you don't have that trait, blessed are you among all people. Waiting is part of the believer's growing process.

*"But they that wait upon the Lord . . ."* **Isaiah 40:31 KJV**

*"There is a way that seems right to a man, but its end is the way to death."*
**Proverbs 16:25 ESV**

Each of us, I'm sure, needs to learn to wait more, and I much more than others. What about you? Is there something that you have asked of the Lord and it seems as though He is slow? God is not slow. He is not slack as some people think but is long suffering, **2 Peter 3:9.** God moves in the fullness of time and at just the right time. God has heard your prayer, so just sit back and rest a while. God is not slow as you seem to think. He is sure.

Think about it. *Selah!*

## Day 29: What Did Jesus Mean By Love Your Enemies?

*"But I say to you who hear, Love your enemies, do good to those who hate you, bless those who curse you, pray for those who abuse you."* **Luke 6:27 ESV**

Who is your neighbor? Who is your enemy? Who is it that curses you? Who is it that lashes out at you for no apparent or valid reason? Who is it that spreads lies about you and says all types of vile things concerning you that are totally untrue? What should you do about it? Do you need to respond with wrath? Where is it in Scripture that we find the charge to form demonstrations against governments? What is our defense against wrong doers on this earth? Do we even have an earthly defender? Does the Bible address these issues? Have you ever thought about it?

What the believer has been commissioned to do on this earth is to carry the Good News to the whole world, **Matthew 28:19-20.** Everyone needs to hear the Good News, and all those people that we come in contact with in our daily lives need to hear it. Those people are our neighbors, **Luke 10:29-37.**

Jesus asked us to show love to those that we meet along the way of life because, love is the icon of God, it is how our neighbors know we are truly Jesus' disciples, **John 13:35.**

As we carry the Good News, we are not to do anything in our own power but rather in the power of the Holy Spirit, **Acts 1:8.** We are to expect opposition as to how we carry out this Great Commission, and we are to understand that our enemy is not flesh and blood. It is not human beings. It is not our neighbors. Our opposition is principalities, the cosmic powers and workers of iniquity everywhere, even in heavenly places, **Ephesians 6:12.**

Remember, God is our ultimate defense but He has authorized governing authorities to unleash His wrath, **Romans 13:1-7; I Peter 2:13-17, 3:8-22, 4:12-19 & 5:6.** Paul and Peter tell us not to resist them but understand that they are the arm of God's wrath. Yes, there will be times when governments will come into direct opposition to our carrying the Good News. At those times, our Biblical word view is that we must obey God rather than man. *" . . . We strictly charged you not to teach in this name, yet here you have filled Jerusalem with your teaching, and you intend to bring this man's blood upon us. But Peter and the apostles answered, 'We must obey God rather than men.' "* **Acts 5:28-29 ESV**

There are many times believers find themselves not opposed by those outside the church but by those inside the church. It is sad to admit but we often find the cancer of fighting, discord, and the seeds of dissention ravaging the church. How is that possible? It is possible when the works of the flesh begin to grow in the church. *"Now the works of the flesh are evident: sexual immorality, impurity, sensuality, idolatry, sorcery, enmity, strife, jealousy, fits of anger, rivalries, dissensions, divisions, envy, drunkenness, orgies, and things like these. I warn you, as I warned you before, that those who do such things will not inherit the kingdom of God."* **Galatians 5:19-21 ESV**

Check those things out.  Those attributes are works of the flesh, not the fruit of the Spirit. The works of the flesh are the enemy of the church.

What are we to do in his fight against principalities and powers?  Suit up!
Put on the Armor and stand, **Ephesians 6:13-18.** *"Resist the devil, and he will flee from you.  Draw near to God, and he will draw near to you."* **James 4:7-8 ESV**

It's up to you and it's up to me.

Think about it. *Selah!*

## Day 30:  Our Two Best Friends

*"Even though I walk through the valley of the shadow of death, I will fear no evil, for you are with me; your rod and your staff, they comfort me.* **Psalm 23:4 ESV**

A missionary, who was living with his family in a Middle East country, was asked by a pastor of a church in the USA: *"Does it frighten you to be living here in the very presence of Islamic terrorism?  Aren't you fearful for your wife and three children?"*  The response of the missionary was, *"No, the most fearful thing to me would be to be somewhere that was thought to be safe but out of the Will of God."*

The safest, and most peaceful place that one can be is in the hand of God, doing His will.  We need not live in fear for the moment.  We are to live in the peace of God that passes all understanding.  We are commanded not to fear the one who can kill the body but unable to kill the soul, we should fear Him who is able to destroy both body and soul, **Matthew 10:28.**

**Psalm 23** is one of the most memorized chapters in the Bible.  At verse 4 comes a promise that when we come to the very moment of great fear in our lives, at the very bottom of uncertainty on this earth, in the valley of death, there is no need for fear.  Why?  Because God is with us as we experience it, and as we experience the threat, God sends us two good friends upon which we can depend, Mister Goodness and Mrs. Mercy.  We can be confident that Goodness and Mercy will not abandon us but will follow us all the days of our lives all the way to the House of the Lord.  They are God's good hand of comfort.

Evil has no hold on us unless we allow it to take a grip. God offers to us comfort in the presence of great evil, and we can be comforted to know that along with Goodness and Mercy is God Himself, who will use His staff of wrath upon the marauders of evil and pulls us to Himself in the face of evil with his staff of care.

The acts of Goodness and Mercy are linked with the kindness of God's gracious heart toward a table of feasting in the face of evil. We are the sheep of His pasture, and we can take comfort in His loving and present voice. We know that voice quite well.

Evil has no lasting hold on us because the Victor is with us and we are His. God has drawn a line in the sand. Satan and his band of terrorists can go no further. God has limited him and empowered us.

So, we all will go through the valley of the shadow of death and many other dark times of uncertainty, but God is with us. His two friends, Goodness and Mercy are placed before us to encourage us.

Think about it. *Selah!*

# Day 31: A Prayer For Our Children

*"And Asa slept with his fathers and was buried with his fathers in the city of David his father, and Jehoshaphat his son reigned in his place."* **1 Kings 15:24 ESV**

*"And Jehoshaphat his son reigned in his place."* Children are an extension of us, their parents. They are what they are, in most part, by how we raised them. More often than not, they caught their values by what they observed, rather than what we verbally taught them.

The older we get the more we understand that life is brief. In **Job 14:1 KJV,** we read, *"Man that is born of a woman is of few days, and full of trouble."* Though brief, we continue to make an impact upon this world through our children. David Jeremiah has commented on the life of a believer in Christ Jesus:

*"It isn't true that when a person dies,* [a believer] *he really dies, because he lives not only in the presence of the Lord, but if he is a Christian, in the children who live after him. And if those children are born into the family of God, they will carry that influence with them throughout their lives and through their children's lives after them."* **David Jeremiah**

How we raise our children is of great importance. The time we spend with them is of most significance. They need quality time, that is true, but the quantity of time we spend with them is of untold value to them. It is in the quantity of time that our children are shaped and molded the most.

The disciples learned by the quantity of time Jesus spent with them. They were taught and affected by the quality, of Jesus' time with them, but their quantity of time spent with Jesus shaped them most. Day after day Jesus remained the same.

Jesus enjoyed the children being around Him, and he didn't want them to have to wait. He wanted them now. He was ready for them. He was upset with the disciples because they thought the time was not convenient for the children to go to Jesus. Jesus told the disciples that the kingdom of heaven was filled with people with child like faith. *"... Let the children come to me; do not hinder them, for to such belongs the kingdom of God"* **Mark 10:14 ESV.**

The challenge is this: parents take time with your children right now. It has been said that there are no dress rehearsals in life and life is as it is, so use it. If you snooze, you lose. God has entrusted our children to us, and we are to make mighty warriors for the Lord Jesus Christ of them. So parents, raise them up in the ways of the Lord! Training is hard. Training takes time and it is long, it is monotonous, and it is frustrating. But they are worth it. Pray for your children.

Think about it. *Selah!*

## Day 32: Though None Go With Me, Still I Will Follow

*"Peter answered him, 'Though they all fall away because of you, I will never fall away!'"* **Matthew 26:33 ESV**

Peter was adamant about what he told Jesus. He wasn't just blowing smoke. Peter meant every word of what he told Jesus, and so did the rest of the disciples at that moment of decision. They all chimed in to be in agreement with Peter. The problem here was not their loyalty to Jesus but the extent of their strength and the understanding of their weakness. Paul would later write, " . . . let anyone who thinks that he stands take heed lest he fall." **1 Corinthians 10:12 ESV**

It was Satan's personal request to Jesus. He wanted Peter, and he was going to wreak havoc upon him; but it was the personal intervention of Jesus on behalf of Peter through His praying specifically for him that mattered. That prayer for Peter by Jesus made all the difference. Jesus knew what was going to happen. Peter did not and, therefore, gave Peter some words of comfort about his future when He said: *". . . but I have prayed for you that your faith may not fail. And when you have turned again, strengthen your brothers."* **Luke 22:32 ESV.** I love those words: *"but I have prayed for you."* Peter and the rest of the disciples thought they knew themselves and the future, but they did not. Jesus was their security, their hope, and their strength for the future.

A song that is frequently used as a song of commitment is *"I Have Decided to Follow Jesus."* I love those words, and I am sure you do also. It is our desire to follow Jesus wherever He may want to lead us, but we need to add a little more to our statement, such as, "Lord,

I have decided to follow You; give me the strength to be able to follow You." It is a certainty that all faithful followers of the Lord Jesus Christ will encounter times of challenge to their commitment. It is as we are in the very act of our commitment to Jesus that we need the faithful prayer of Jesus to strengthen us and enable us.

Today we hear of companies that were considered, "too big to fail," but they did fail. We must understand that if we think we are too big to fail, and we think we can stand on our own strength of commitment, then we better take heed: *"Therefore let anyone who thinks that he stands take heed lest he fall"*, 1 **Corinthians 10:12 ESV.** If we think we are strong, we better think again. All that a believer does must be done in the power and strength of the Lord. He is our strength. We are no better than Peter and the rest of the disciples.

Place your trust in God, not in man. God is able to do anything and can do it at any time He chooses. Remember, we are an extension of the Hand of God, not the hand of God. We cannot do all things, but we can do all things through Jesus Christ. We have the power of God upon us, but we are not the power of God. The Good News is the result of all that God has done and not our doing. It is the strength of the prayer of Jesus that will make all the difference in us and in others.

At the Second International Congress on World Evangelism in 1989 in the *Manila Manifesto* is found this statement:

*"The Scriptures declare that God Himself is the chief evangelist. For the Spirit of God is the Spirit of truth, love, holiness and power, and evangelism is impossible without*

*Him. It is He who anoints the messenger, confirms the Word, prepares the hearer, convinces the sinful, enlightens the blind, gives life to the dead, enables us to repent and believe, unites us to the body of Christ, assures us that we are God's children, leads us into Christ-like character and service, and sends us out in turn to be Christ's witnesses. In all this the Holy Spirit's main preoccupation is to glorify Jesus Christ by showing Him to us and forming Him in us."*

Though none go with me, the Holy Spirit is with me, and through Him I maintain the power to do that which He has called me to do. With the Holy Spirit by my side, yes, I will follow.

Go in the strength and power of the Lord. It is Jesus who has sent us, and we have answered His call. It is the Holy Spirit who enables us, and we are enabled to do what we do for the glory of Christ Jesus.

Like Peter and the disciples, our desire is to follow Christ. Our Passion is to obey His call; our ambition is to go to the harvest in the strength of the Lord.

Think about it. *Selah!*

## Day 33: This Old House

*" 'Death is swallowed up in victory.' 'O death, where is your victory? O death where is your sting?' " The sting of death is sin, and the power of sin is the law. But thanks be to God who gives us the victory through our Lord Jesus Christ."*
**1 Corinthians 15:54-56 ESV**

The person who has taken Jesus Christ as his personal Savior has had his sins cast into the sea of God's chosen forgetfulness. Those sins are as removed from God "as far as the east is from the west," **Psalm 103:12.** Those sins have been covered by the righteousness of Jesus Christ, **2 Corinthians 5:21.** The reward for this act of faith is eternal life in exchange for eternal death, **John 3:16-21.** For those people this mortal body will be exchanged for an immortal one formed by the very hand of God Himself.

*"For we know that when this earthly tent we live in is taken down (that is, when we die and leave this earthly body), we will have a house in heaven, an eternal body made for us by God himself and not by human hands."* **2 Corinthians 5:1 NLT**

When a loved one dies, it is not the end of that person's life; it is the beginning of life eternal, the life that Jesus has made known to us. This is the great plan of God for mankind. He wants as many as would believe, to believe, and that is why He is seemingly slow in His returning to earth for us. His reason for patiently waiting is because he is giving everyone all the time needed to make his or her decision for Him, and He doesn't want anyone to perish or spend eternity in eternal death. Eternal death is fearful, but eternal life is eagerly anticipated.

Read this poem. It reminds me that *God has a plan not for our harm but for our good,* **Jeremiah 29:11.**

## THERE IS NO DEATH

*There is a plan far greater than the plan you know;*
*There is a landscape broader than the one you see.*
*There is a heaven where storm-tossed souls may go-*
*You call it death - we, immortality.*

\

*You call it death - this seeming endless sleep;*
*We call it birth - the soul at last set free.*
*Tis hampered not by time or space - you weep,*
*Why weep at death? Tis immortality.*

*Farewell, dear voyageur - 'twill not be long.*
*Your work is done - now may peace rest with thee.*
*Your kindly thoughts and deeds - they will live on.*
*This is not death - 'tis immortality.*

*Farewell, dear voyageur - the river winds and turns;*
*The cadence of your song wafts near to me,*
*And now you know the thing that all men learn:*
*There is no death - there's immortality.*
**Unknown**

I don't know who wrote this poem. The credit has been give to the "Unknown." I guess it's like the tomb of the Unknown Soldier.

We don't know who it is that is held there, but we are so thankful for all those who fought with him, and we give honor to all with the inscription, "Unknown." Though unknown to us, they are well known by God.

Think about it. *Selah!*

## Day 34:  Repentance?  What Does That Mean?

*"There were some present at that very time who told him about the Galileans whose blood Pilate had mingled with their sacrifices. And he answered them, 'Do you think that these Galileans were worse sinners than all the other Galileans, because they suffered in this way? No, I tell you; but unless you repent, you will all likewise perish. Or those eighteen on whom the tower in Siloam fell and killed them: do you think that they were worse offenders than all the others who lived in Jerusalem? No, I tell you; but unless you repent, you will all likewise perish."* **Luke 13:1-3 ESV**

This was a tragic event that took place at the Tower of Siloam.  Exactly where that was is not definitely known, but it was well known at the time that Jesus was speaking here. These Galileans were in Jerusalem worshiping.  Pilate, for some reason, had slaughtered these eighteen people while they were in the very act of worship.

The temple, which was supposed to be a refuge of peace and safety, had become a snare for slaughter. The blood of the sacrificed animal was mingled with the blood of the worshipers. They had come all the way from Galilee just to worship, and then this happens.

The crowd wondered why.  They probably thought that the reason was that these Galileans were being punished for their sins unknown by other worshipers that day.  The opinion of the Judean Jews was that the Galilean Jews were not as good as they were.  Remember the response?  Can anything good come from Nazareth? Nazareth was in Galilee.

Jesus knew their thoughts, and His response was unexpected as He told them: No, they are not worse off than you are, unless you repent you too will perish as they did, **Luke 13:1-3.** They would perish suddenly and unexpectedly. You see, repentance was the answer for sin, not the blame. The blame is that all have sinned and come short of the glory of God, **Romans 3:23.** The tragedy of the blame was not that they were killed but that they had not repented. They traveled the long road to Jerusalem to worship, but the desire for worship and the act of worship in itself did not save them. Repentance was what was needed to save them. Jesus was saying that unless the listeners repented, they too were on the road to death, eternal death, and would die in their sin.

What is repentance? Shortly put, repentance is turning around. Repentance is admitting that you are on the wrong road, that you have been all your life, and therefore, you make a change of direction in your life. You repent of your sin. You turn around and find the answer is on that new road, the road of forgiveness. Forgiveness is as Alexander Pope wrote in <u>Essay on Criticism</u>:

> *"Ah ne'er a Thirst of Glory boast,*
> *Nor in the critic let man be lost!*
> *Good-nature and good-sense must ever join*
> *To err (sin) is human, to forgive is divine."*

Forgiveness is for God only to offer, and offering is what Jesus was doing. He was offering forgiveness for sin as a reward for repentance of sin. Forgiveness is something that can only be received by stopping, turning around, and having a change of direction. The believer must have faith and trust in Jesus in order to receive forgiveness. Jesus is the only way and the only one in whom I can have hope for forgiveness. He is the sacrifice, the only sacrifice for sin. He is the final sacrifice for sin.

*"But when Christ had offered for all time a single sacrifice for sins he sat down at the right hand of God, waiting from that time until his enemies should be made a footstool for his feet. For by a single offering he has perfected for all time those who are being sanctified."* **Hebrews 10:12-14 ESV**

- Worship does not bring forgiveness of sin;
- Good deeds are not rewarded with forgiveness for sin;
- Christian families, and Christian nations do not secure forgiveness of sin;
- Faithful service is not the requirement for forgiveness;

Repentance is the first step and involved with repentance is our believing what Jesus has said. If you will repent, you will not perish but have everlasting life. **John 3:16**

Repentance is turning around.

Think about it. *Selah!*

## Day 35: Commencement

*"You then, my child, be strengthened by the grace that is in Christ Jesus, and what you have heard from me in the presence of many witnesses entrust to faithful men who will be able to teach others also."* **2 Timothy 2:1-2 ESV**

Graduation! All students, high school, college, trade school or whatever the training school may be, are looking forward to that day, and so do parents. But for the most part to all who are involved and are eager for that day to arrive, there is a huge misunderstanding or misconception of that day. For some reason, we tend to think graduation is the completion, but the truth is, it is actually the beginning of things that really matter. It is called commencement, and commencement means that things are about to commence, to start, to begin, not end. For the parent, the big bucks are about to begin.

The plans are being studied, the map is being plotted, and the preparation for the life trip is being made. After all that has been done, we get into the car and begin on our trek in life. As we travel down the road, we remember the things that we have been taught and find that information to be invaluable as we roll down life's highway.

For the Believer, we not only have the experience of information, and the backing of friends and family, but we have the GPS of the Holy Spirit. At times we get off track and we hear, "recalculating, recalculating", but never are we abandoned, the signal is always strong. Our job is to listen, obey and go. "This is the way, walk in it." **Isaiah 30:21 ESV**

Jesus told His disciples that He was going to prepare a place for them and that where He was going, they could not come at that time, but He would be coming back for them. For the time being He was leaving His GPS, the Holy Spirit, with them and He would teach them and lead them in The Way.

It's interesting that the followers of Jesus were known as *The Way*. "*But this I confess to you, that according the Way, which they call a sect, I worship the God of our fathers, believing everything laid down by the Law and written in the Prophets.*"
**Acts 24:14 ESV**

As we commence down the road of life, we can be confident that our Guide will neither leave us nor forsake us on the way, as we remain in The Way, representing The Way, The Truth and The Life to all that we meet. What we have learned, we teach others and make disciples of others so that they may, in turn, make disciples.

Never give in, never give up, and never turn back!

Think about it. *Selah!*

## Day 36:  Where Is Your Faith?

*"Now faith is the substance of things hoped for, the evidence of things not seen."*
**Hebrews 11:1 KJV**

If you have good health, that in itself is not a sign of great faith.
If you have great wealth, that also in itself is not a sign of great faith.
If you have no worry in life, that is not proof of great faith.

Your faith is confirmed by your total trust and reliance and is magnified by your obedience to Jesus.  Do you trust Him with your life?

Your faith is demonstrated as you may go through times of poor health.  It is your faith that relies upon Jesus in your time of insufficiency.   It is your faith that is observed by those around you. The peace that you display as you go through times of stress and overwhelming opposition of all types verifies your faith and shouts to all who know you that your faith is strong.

Faith is the SUBSTANCE, the basic make up, the foundation of your life and how you live. Faith is the reason for the way you think.  It is your mindset, your confidence, and your peace in waiting for what you are hoping.   Faith is the EVIDENCE you have for your confidence and happy life because you know God answers your prayers and supplies your present and future needs. Faith is the proof for your case in believing God.  Faith is not your religion; it is your life in Christ.

The sign of your faith is the fruit you display every day, not a bumper sticker. The Bible tells us that it is by our love and fruits we are known. Faith is displayed through our love, joy, peace, patience, kindness, goodness, faithfulness, gentleness, and self-control, **Galatians 5:22.**

So, what evidence do you have on display for your faith? Do you have the basic make up for living a life of faith? If you have little faith, seek for greater faith. Ask for greater faith. *"Lord, I believe; help thou mine unbelief,"* **Mark 9:24 KJV.** Don't doubt; believe, hope, and live in faith.

Think about it. *Selah!*

## Day 37: The Cross: This Is The King Of The Jews

*"Pilate also wrote an inscription and put it on the cross. It read, 'Jesus of Nazareth, the King of the Jews.' "* **John 19:19 ESV**

What did people think about Jesus?

**Pilate:** "Do you not know that I have authority to release you and authority to crucify you?" **John 19:10 ESV**

**Jesus**: You have no authority but that which was given to you. **John 19:11**

**The Crowd:** "He saved others; let him save himself," **Luke 23:35 ESV**

**The Unrepentant Thief:** "Are you not the Christ? Save yourself and us!"
 **Luke 23:39 ESV**

**Soldiers:** "If you are the King of the Jews, save yourself!" **Luke 23:37 ESV**

**Jesus:** "Father, if you are willing, remove this cup from me. Nevertheless, not my will, but yours, be done." **Luke 22:42 ESV**
"I did not come to the world to judge the world but to save the world." **John 12:47**

- The cross was a tool of the Roman government.
- The cross was for the payment of our sin debt.
- Sin against God was the crime.
- Jesus was the payment, the atonement, the Savior for the crime of mankind.

- The Father was the designer of the plan.
- The plaque on the cross was the official proclamation of who Jesus was.

Jesus could have done what everyone was shouting. He could have saved himself, but He didn't need to be saved. We did, they did, and this world still needs to be saved. If He had come down from the cross, He would have saved himself, but He would not have saved others. He would have failed in his mission and His plan of redemption for the world. But Jesus never fails, ever!

The cross was God's predetermined plan, and it was the will of the Father. The Roman nails did not hold Him there on the cross. His love for us kept Him there.

The repentant thief on the cross had it right that day. He asked of Jesus, "remember me when you come into your kingdom," **Luke 23:42 ESV**, and the answer was, "today you will be with me in Paradise," **Luke 23:43 ESV.**

Think about it. *Selah!*

### Day 38:  Be A Light For The Light Into The Darkness

Don't hide your light under a basket!  Instead, put it on a stand and let it shine for all.  **Matthew 5:15**

I like this quote from Jay Sekulow of The American Center for Law and Justice (ACLJ):  *"Jesus died for you publicly, so, don't live for Him privately."*

Jesus said it this way:  *"Nor do they light a lamp and put it under a basket, but on a lampstand, and it gives light to all who are in the house.  Let your light so shine before men, that they may see your good works and glorify your Father in heaven."* **Matthew 5:15-16 NKJV**

Jesus said of Himself: " . . . *I am the light of the world . . ."* **John 8:12 NKJV.**
Jesus demonstrated it by placing Himself on a stand (the cross), and all throughout history, He has brightly shone for the whole world to see that Light.

How are you letting your light reflect the Light of the World?  We are not to explain **The Light**, we are just to be a light and let our light shine before men.  **The Light** says it all.  **The Light** cannot be overlooked, cannot be denied, and cannot be hidden unless it is put under a basket.

Drop your basket and hold up the Light.

Think about it. *Selah!*

# Day 39: I Would, But . . .

*"Let the spiritually dead bury their own dead! Your duty is to go and preach about the Kingdom of God."* **Luke 9:60 NLT**

If time was no factor, if money was not a consideration, and if ability had no bearing, what would you do? I'm sure something big comes into your mind, but let me inject one more factor to that question: If these things were true for you, what would you do for the Lord Jesus Christ; what would you do for God?

Here is the kicker; none of those factors are a factor in our doing what God calls us to do. Our only factor is our response to His, call and it should be: *"Yes, Lord, I will."* Your question to me might be, "How can I say that?" It may seem totally irrational and even unnatural.

You know what? It is irrational and unnatural. It is totally supernatural. Our success is a God thing, or it is a God calling in your life. Not to take those things into consideration takes faith! It takes great faith to do what God calls you to do. It takes great faith in God's Word to just go with no questions asked. It takes total obedience, and it requires no looking for excuses or no looking back after you begin and run into opposition.

Paul writes in **Philippians 4:13 & 19** that it is through Christ that we are able to do anything and it is God himself who has promised to supply all our needs. All that is required of us to do is to do that which He has called us to do. He alone is our supply and our confidence.

In **Luke 9:59,** a follower of Jesus told him that he would follow him wherever he might go, but first he wanted to go bury his father. That seems reasonable, doesn't it, but Jesus was not wanting a reasonable or natural response to his request to follow him. He was looking for obedience. Jesus informs his follower: *"Let the spiritually dead bury their own dead! Your duty is to go and preach about the Kingdom of God."* **Luke 9:60 NLT**

Now, back to you. What was it that came to your mind when pondering my proposal regarding obeying God? If that thought was a personal call of God in your life, then you must do it. Don't allow thoughts of why you can't do it hinder you. Think of why you can do it. You can do it if God is calling you, because He is the one who empowers you. It is He who is your supplier. God is the one who holds time in His hands. What God wants from you is obedience.

Think about it. *Selah!*

# Day 40: What Did You Do?

*"But Samuel replied, 'What is more pleasing to the Lord: your burnt offerings and sacrifices or your obedience to his voice? Listen! Obedience is better than sacrifice, and submission is better than offering the fat of rams.' "* **1 Samuel 15:22 NLT**

Someone has said, *"Nothing is worse than being born and dying without much in between."* Doing is important. Being involved is beneficial to a movement, but what you are doing, how you are doing it, and with whom you are involved in the process determine the quality of your success. It isn't the knowledge that you may lack that keeps you from being successful; it is what you do with the knowledge that you have that makes you successful..

Israel's first king, Saul, was an impressive young man. Though Saul wasn't looking for a position, the position came looking for him. Saul was head and shoulders above the rest of the young men of his day. He was impressive in stature yet humble, obedient, likeable, as well as strong. He had the qualities that were needed to make a positive difference as a leader of the people. But Saul did not remain that way. Something happened on his road in life that changed this humble young man. What ruined Saul was that his opinion of himself and his ambition changed after he was placed into leadership. Saul began to think he really was head and shoulders above everyone else and that he could do what he wanted to do. He began to think he just needed to appease everyone and that he could then do what would please himself. When Samuel questioned his actions that day, he thought he could appease him by saying, "I'm sorry, would you please forgive me?" He figured he would just ask for forgiveness and everyone would be happy. He wasn't sorry though.

God gave Saul specific instructions, but he refused to obey God. He figured he would just give a sacrifice for his disobedience. Samuel's response to Saul's sacrifice was: *"Obedience is better than sacrifice,"* **I Samuel 15:22 NLT**. The apostle Paul said it like this: *"Well then, should we keep on sinning so that God can show us more and more of his wonderful grace? Of course not! Since we have died to sin, how can we continue to live in it?* **Romans 6:1-2 NLT**

Obedience is important if you want to be a successful follower of Jesus Christ. It is incumbent upon you to live a life of obedience to the Word of God and do His will, not do your own will or do it your way.

We have upon us the righteousness of Christ, and we are His ambassadors. We should live honorably in His righteousness. Success for the follower of Christ is not what we do but how we do God's will. The measuring stick of success is the presence of the fruit of the Spirit in our lives, not the amount of time we spend asking forgiveness for the works of the flesh.

Think about it. *Selah!*

## Day 41:  Whatever Happens, Keep Going

*"But whatever gain I had, I counted as loss for the sake of Christ.  Indeed, I count everything as loss because of the surpassing worth of knowing Christ Jesus my Lord."*
**Philippians 3:7-8 ESV**


Have you ever wondered, why are you where you are? Have you ever taken the time to consider how you got to where you are right now?  Was it God who led you to where you are or was it your own ambition?

If it was from your own ambition, then it was by your own power and by your own ability that you have arrived at this location with the situation you find yourself in.  If it is God who led you to where you are, then do you know why He led you here?  Whether the situation is good or bad is not the question in your estimation.  The reason you are where you are is to be the voice of God with the power of God and to be His witness and His ambassador. You are not the Holy Spirit who convicts and changes people; you are the witness with a message. You have come to make disciples of those who obey God's voice.

Here is a Scriptural truth: God did not call you where you are for you to get mad and leave, or to settle down and live out your life in superficial peace and comfort. God's command is to go, and He expects you to obey. You must follow where He leads, but don't move until He leads.  While you are where you are, the Holy Spirit is giving you on-the-job training.  With each experience, you gain an increased ability to hear the still small voice of the Holy Spirit to teach and comfort others in greater ways.

God wants us to be obedient. We have nothing to prove other than being obedient. God wants us to obey Him, not to prove that we are good sons and daughters, but so that we can see that He is a good Father who loves His children and provides for them.

If things aren't going as you feel they should or if things are wonderful, you are not through nor is God through with you. He is equipping you to do more and in more ways. We are not on this earth to quit or settle down. We stop at the gates of heaven. We settle down in heaven. Until we cross the finish line, we need to keep going.

I don't want my life to be lived without the help of the Holy Spirit.

*If you have no need of help, why would you need a helper?*
*If you are already comfortable, why would you need a comforter?*

Don't stop now, don't slow down, keep going, never say quit, never say can't, never give up, and never give in. Listen, obey and keep going.

Think about it. *Selah!*

# Day 42:  Teach Us To Pray

*"Now Jesus was praying in a certain place, and when he finished, one of his disciples said to him, 'Lord teach us to pray, as John taught his disciples.' "* **Luke 11:1 ESV**

Jesus taught his disciples many things but the one thing that they requested of Him to teach them was, *"Teach us to pray."* The request to be taught to pray was inspired by their witnessing Jesus pray. The prayers of Jesus were powerful, impassioned, and personal.  I am sure to hear Jesus pray was a marvelous thing.

The disciples wanted to be able to pray in the same way that they heard Jesus pray. John the Baptist, after all, had taught his disciples to pray, and they desired Jesus to teach them to pray, not like John the Baptist, but like He prayed.

When Jesus prayed to His Father, it was as though they were listening in on a private conversation, and that was true.  Jesus honored their request and began with a model prayer.  The first words of the model prayer were "Our Father" because He was their Father also. He was a good Father, and He was listening to every word they said as a good Father would.  Man is most happy when he is talking to his Father, to his Creator.

The French mathematician Blaise Pascal, father of the modern theory of probability, scientist, writer, and Christian philosopher, wrote:

> *"If man is not made for God,*
> *Why is he only happy in God.*
> *If man is made for God,*
> *Why is he so opposed to God."*

The poet George Hebert of Wales penned these words:

*"Lord, hear!*
*Shall He that made the ear not hear?"*

We are the children of God and He, our Father and Creator, made us for communication with Him. We communicate through prayer and the reading of His Word. God's ear is sensitive to our voice, and He hears our voice.

So pray or talk with your Father for He is a good Father who, from His good hand desires, to meet our need. From His loving ear, He hears our prayers of need, thanksgiving, and praise, and from His loving heart He offers to us eternal life.

Think about it. *Selah!*

## Day 43: I Just Can't Get It All Done!

*"And Moses said to the people, 'Fear not, stand firm, and see the salvation of the Lord, which he will work for you today. For the Egyptians whom you see today, you shall never see again.'"* **Exodus 14:13 ESV**

Have you ever been given a job or taken on a task that you felt completely incapable of completing? Have you ever begun a task in which the more you became involved in it, the more involved it became, and you came to the point you realized that you were just not capable of completing it by yourself? I think we all have at one time or another.

When you can't get it done, get done what you can and are capable of doing, and leave the rest to God. God is more than capable of doing all the rest. Not only is He capable of doing the rest:

　　1.　He invites us to come to Him boldly to get it done. **Hebrews 4:16**

　　2.　We "can do all things through Christ who strengthens" us, **Philippians 4:13 NKJV.** "And my God shall supply all your need according to his riches in glory by Christ Jesus." **Philippians 4:19 NKVJ**

　　3.　He is "able to do exceeding abundantly above all that we ask or think," **Ephesians 3:20 KJV**

4. Ask and you shall receive. You do not have because you have not asked.
**1 John 3:22 & 5:14-15**

5. You ask and receive not because you ask selfishly. **James 4:2 -3**

These are all promises from God to do all that is needed in serving him.

God does not ask us to be able to do things. He asks that we do all things through Christ Jesus. Personal power, prowess, or ability is not a requirement, but weakness and dependence upon God is. God does not require us to be intelligent. He wants us to be obedient. He does not want us to ever fear, because fear is doubt. He wants us to be victors and conquerors through Him.

No, we can't get it all done. If we could, it is a mere human thing that can be done outside of God. God wants us to do our best and then leave Him the rest. Stand firm and see!

Think about it. *Selah!*

## Day 44:  Why Do They Hate Me?

*"Remember the word that I said to you: 'A servant is not greater than his master.' If they persecuted me, they will also persecute you, if they kept my word, they will also keep yours."* **John 15:20 ESV**

At Easter, vast numbers of crowds gather to exclaim, "Christ is risen!  He is risen indeed!"  Sanctuaries are filled, choirs sing, and pulpits proclaim the Gospel message.  St. Peter's Square is filled with thousands as they listen to the words of the Pope with joy in their hearts and praise upon their lips.

As all of this happens from year to year, a stark reminder of the words of Jesus in the passage above was realized on Easter, 2015, in a remote village in Kenya.  A friend of mine, Dr. Jon Duncan sent this to me in an email: "Only twelve worshipers were in attendance that Easter. An Associated Press reporter was there and noted that in Garissa, Kenya the pastor shared: 'We have to sing the song with a happy voice.'  The congregation of twelve was missing 147 of their friends who were killed by Islamic terrorists.  Yet, they sang with fervor:

*"O happy day, O happy day,*
*When Jesus washed,*
*When my Jesus washed,*
*When my Jesus Washed*
*He washed my sins away!"*

*He taught me how to watch and pray,*
*And live rejoicing every day*
*O happy day, O happy day*
*When my Jesus washed*
*All my sins away!*

Although small in number, their conviction shouts loudly of the reality of the resurrection. Their courage and faith inspired me beyond words." - **Jon Duncan**

How blessed is the church in the western world and how thankful we should be that we can worship freely at this time. But I am afraid the time is soon coming and perhaps is even now at hand that this blessing will be replaced by persecution here as it is in the rest of the world.

Persecution is not something new or unexpected for the Christian and follower of Jesus Christ. It is a way of life. It is how life has always been and always will be until Jesus returns for His church. The world hated Jesus, and because they hated Him, they can do nothing but hate His followers. It is the fact of life before eternal life.

Our problem is not with Islam, the atheists, or governments, but with principalities and powers in high and even heavenly places. The world is only following the dictates of its leader, Satan.

*"Have I not commanded you? Be strong and courageous. Do not be frightened, and do not be dismayed, for the Lord your God is with you wherever you go."* **Joshua 1:9 ESV**

Take courage, be not dismayed, fear not, be strong, be courageous, stand and put on the Armor of God. **Ephesians 6:10-20**

Think about it. *Selah!*

## Day 45:  God Cannot Lie, But You Can

*"God is not man that he should lie, or a son of man that he should change . . ."*
**Numbers 23:19 ESV**

Do you know people that you question everything they say?  Can people rely on what you tell them?  If you need help, you always seek out those people whose word you can rely upon.  There is comfort that comes with truth.  Jesus is The Truth, The Light and the Way.

In **Psalm 103:11-13 & 17 ESV** we read: *"For as the heavens are above the earth, so great is His steadfast love toward those who fear him; as far as the east is from the west, so far does he remove our transgressions from us. As a father shows compassion to his children, so the Lord shows compassion to those who fear him . . . .  But the steadfast love of the Lord is from everlasting to everlasting on those who fear him, and his righteousness to children's children".*

If God forgives you, what right do you have to bring up something that does not exist?  Is God lying?  I don't think so!  Remember the length of His forgiveness.  It is as far as the east is from the west, not the north from the south. God is the one who is offering forgiveness and He cannot lie.  You are the one who is questioning a God who cannot lie.

Who are you to question God?

Think about it.  *Selah!*

## Day 46: The Battle And The Fight

*"When Joshua was near the town of Jericho, he looked up and saw a man standing in front him with sword in hand. Joshua went up to him and demanded, 'Are you friend or foe?' 'Neither one,' he replied. 'I am the commander of the LORD's army.' At this, Joshua fell with his face to the ground in reverence. 'I am at your command,' Joshua said. 'What do you want your servant to do?' "* **Joshua 5:13-14 NLT**

The believer will have trouble, he will have battles to fight as he is in a war. But the war is not with people. It is with evil. The question we have is where is the fight and with whom is the battle. What are the rules of engagement?

Joshua knew where the battle was that day. It was Jericho. Joshua was preparing for battle when he was confronted with a man with a sword in his hand. Who was this man and why was he there? Joshua's challenge was: Are you for us or against us?

The response was: I'm not for you or against you. I am the commander of the Lord's Angel army. Whoa! What do you do when you are confronted with an Angel with his sword drawn? The correct answer would be to fall down and ask for instruction. This is not the time for battle. It is the time for instruction.

In our lives there are times of engagement and times of prayer and dependence upon God. I heard my dad, **Glenn E. Thomas,** say this: *"What happens when you quit fighting? God steps in."* When we are obedient, God's strength is most powerful in our lives. We must stand, trust, and obey for there is no other way.

Mankind has many implements of battle but victory comes at the hand of God. *"The horse is made ready for the day of battle, but the victory belongs to the Lord,"* **Proverbs 21:31 ESV.** *"The Lord will fight for you, and you have only to be silent,"* **Exodus 14:14 ESV.**

Satan is our enemy and not people. His strategies are carefully planned and powerful. We are not able to stand against them, but God is more than able. Alan Redpath has written:

*"Satan's attacks on the child of God are always carefully planned out, counter-attacks on the devil seldom are based on any strategy at all. Too often we trust in half-heated and hot-headed methods, which end in defeat and tragedy for us."* **Allen Redpath,** <u>Victorious Christian Living,</u> Pg. 149.

God needs no counter attack. He fights to win and win he will. Do not have anything to do with unfruitful works against Satan. Just put on your armor and stand. Leave the fight to the Lord. He is the victor and the conqueror.

The believer will have many battles. We must understand where the battle is, and we must know whom we are fighting as we go obeying the command of the Commander of the Lord's army. When we come to the end of our resources, it is then that we must stand still and let God step in. When we quit our personal fight, we are not giving up. We are letting the Victor step in.

What is your battle right now?  Does it seem that you are losing?  On whom are you depending?  Your horses of battle may be ready for battle but the battle belongs to the Lord.  So, stand still and see the glory of God.  *"The horse is made ready for the day of battle, but the victory belongs to the Lord."* **Proverbs 21:31 ESV**   *"The Lord will fight for you, and you have only to be silent."* **Exodus 14:14 ESV**

Give your battle to God and be faithful and obedient to God's Word.  The battle is actually won, and you are more than a conqueror.

Think about it. *Selah!*

# Day 47: Letters Of Encouragement

*"For I long to see you, that I may impart to you some spiritual gift to strengthen you--that is, that we may be mutually encouraged by each other's faith, both yours and mine."* **Romans 1:11-12 ESV**

Do you enjoy receiving mail? Sometimes we call it "snail-mail." I do and I always have enjoyed receiving both expected and unexpected mail. The best type of mail is handwritten mail. With it you know the sender has given you a sample of himself or herself. I read handwritten letters more than once and have many times kept them and cherished them. I remember enjoying the perfumed letters sent to me by my wife, Bobbie. I enjoyed everything about each letter, from her penmanship to the upside-down stamp that was purposefully placed there and meant, *"I love you."* We all, I believe, enjoy receiving handwritten mail. The Apostle Paul knew the significance of writing personal letters with his own hand. Most of his letters were dictated and written by a scribe or a friend. Notice his reference in **Philemon 17 - 19 ESV** *"So if you consider me your partner, receive him as you would receive me. If he has wronged you at all, or owes you anything, charge that to my account. I, Paul, write this with my own hand: I will repay it--to say nothing of your owing me even your own self."*

May I challenge you to be an encourager to your family, friends and acquaintances? A personal letter written in your own hand means something and makes a difference in others' lives.

Think about it. *Selah!*

### Day 48: Pray Specifically

*"But when you pray, go into your room and shut the door and pray to your Father who is in secret. And your Father who sees in secret will reward you."* **Matthew 6:6 ESV**

Prayer is a personal thing between you and your heavenly Father. Jesus told his disciples to pray privately in **Matthew 6:6.** He told them to ask for specific needs in **John 14:13-14.** The writer of Hebrews tells us to come boldly to God in prayer in **Hebrews 4:16**; and in **James 4:2-3,** we are informed that the reason we don't have what we may desire is because we have either not asked, or we have asked with wrong motives.

God is a personal God and He wants us to personally ask Him for our specific needs and ask for any good and right desire that we might have. A request doesn't have to be spiritual, but the desire needs to be a good and right desire. As a parent enjoys fulfilling the good and right desires of our children, so God loves to supply our desires.

What God wants us to do is ask and ask specifically in prayer because He wants to answer our specific prayer with that specific need. *"At that time you won't need to ask me for anything. I tell you the truth, you will ask the Father directly, and he will grant your request because you use my name. You haven't done this before. Ask using my name, and you will receive, and you will have abundant joy."* **John 16:23-24 NLT**

When we receive a specific request, we are filled with joy. The Father is filled with joy also because we asked for a specific thing and we knew that we would receive it.

If we pray in general terms, God answers in general terms. If we pray specifically, God answers with specificity, and we have great joy. God does not need to be informed of our needs because He already knows them, **Matthew 6:8**. He does not need to be reminded of a request because He provides the request at the right time, not at just anytime. He does not need to be challenged in order to act because He has already enacted His plan for our good, **Jeremiah 29:11**; and He had it planned and written down for us before the world was made, **Psalm 139:16**.

My challenge to you is to pray specifically. I want you to see God's hand in your life vividly. Now, one more thing: don't pray for the missionaries around the world, pray for that specific missionary in the world. When you see your prayer answered, then praise God with a joyful heart! He specifically answered your personal prayer.

Think about it. *Selah!*

# Day 49:  Worship In One Accord

*"What then, brothers?  When you come together, each one has a hymn, a lesson, a revelation, a tongue, or an interpretation.  Let all things be done for the building up."*
**1 Corinthians 14:26 ESV**

Worship is a one-on-one thing.  Simply put, worship is when I fix my eye on my great God and lift up my praise and thanksgiving in honor and glory to God alone. Even when worship is done corporately, it is still one worshiper to one God.  If we are alone, we fix our eyes upon God.  If we are with multitudes united in worship, we fix our eyes upon God.  Worship is always done to an audience of one.

What genuine worship looks like is just God and I.  What God expects and deserves is honor, glory, and majesty in worship for He is holy and He is worthy of such praise. We all have personal preferences and ideas of how we prefer to worship.  It is good to have personal ideas of how we worship in that worship is personal, but it is never good or right to impose our preferences of worship upon another worshiper.

We are not the judge of the genuine worship of others, because genuine worship comes from the heart, and we do not know the heart of others.  God is the judge who knows the heart and true thoughts of everyone, and He knows our spirit.

Contemporary, traditional, robes, suits or blue jeans; they make no difference to God for the heart is the main thing.  True worshipers worship in spirit and in truth.

*"But the hour is coming, and is now here, when the true worshipers will worship the Father in spirit and truth, for the Father is seeking such people to worship him. God is spirit, and those who worship him must worship in spirit and truth."* **John 4:23-24 ESV**

Be genuine in your worship, not preferential. Be true and honoring to God and worship him. *"Let all things be done for the building up."* **1 Corinthians 14:26 ESV**

Think about it. *Selah!*

## Day 50:  From The Best-Known Sinner In Town, To The Best-Known Witness In Town

*"Many Samaritans from that town believed in him because of the woman's testimony. 'He told me all that I ever did'."* **John 4:39 ESV**

Your testimony is powerful. How you live shouts boldly into the lives of those around you. We might not want to admit it but what we do matters, and it matters to everyone. What we do and say will involve everyone who knows us. They may know us well, they may know us casually, or they may know us by face only. You can be certain of this that we are being watched, and we are being evaluated. What we do matters.

What we do gives credibility to whatever we say or refutes whatever we say. If we live carelessly before others, as though no one else matters to us or we could care less as to what anyone else may think, then the opposite is true. What we say to them matters nothing to others in the world. They could care less of what we say.

In **John 4:7-18,** it is recorded where Jesus met a Samaritan woman who was well known in her town. She was well known for her sin. Those who knew of her knew of her for her sin. When Jesus met her He asked if she would do something for Him, to draw a cup of water from the well for him. She tells him that she was unable to draw the water for Jesus. Jesus' response was: "I can give you water to drink that will satisfy for eternity." I think her response was a bit sarcastic: "Is that right? Well, then give me some of that so I wont be thirsty anymore." Jesus further engages her in conversation with the request: *"Go, call your husband, and come here."*

*"I have no husband,"* **John 4:16-17 ESV,** was her response.

Now Jesus could be real with her. Her response mattered to Him. Jesus added, you are correct to say you don't have "a" husband because you actually have had five husbands, and the person that you are living with right now is not your husband, **John 4:17-18.**

Everybody knew that, but Jesus was a stranger. How did He know it? Jesus knew it because He was the Messiah, the Christ, the promised one. Her life changed at that meeting and now she would begin a new life in Christ. Her first action was to go tell everyone she knew, *"Come, see a man who told me all that I ever did. Can this be the Christ?"* **John 4:29 ESV**

This was a great turning point in her life. Everything changed. At this point she became known for being a witness for the Christ, the Messiah, her Savior. At this point what she did would make a positive difference in the lives of those she was around, and for many it was an eternal difference. Her testimony was no longer, "Come to my house," but *"Come, see a man who told me all that I ever did. Can this be the Christ?"* **John 4:29 ESV.** Yes, it was the Christ!

What about your life? Does your life matter for the good of those around you? What you do matters after all. What is your testimony?

*"Many Samaritans from that town believed in him because of the woman's testimony. 'He told me all that I ever did'."* **John 4:39 ESV**

Think about it. *Selah!*

## Day 51: The Purpose Of God's Grace and Mercy

*"Therefore, laying aside all malice, all deceit, hypocrisy, envy, and all evil speaking, as new born babes, desire the pure, milk of the word, that you may grow thereby, if indeed you have tasted that the Lord is gracious."* **1 Peter 2:1-3 NKJV**

Jesus came to this earth to pay the penalty for sin, to be the pure and holy sacrifice for sin. He was the only sacrifice that could be made for sin. It took a pure and holy Son of God, the begotten of the Father, to be able to satisfy the pure and holy God. His sacrifice made it possible for mankind to be found holy, righteous, and acceptable before the Father. It was the holiness and righteousness of Jesus that brought all this together. He did it all for all who would believe in Him, by repenting of their sin and taking His righteousness upon them, and, therefore, becoming as righteous and holy as Jesus is. *"For our sake he made him to be sin who knew no sin, so that in him we might become the righteousness of God."* **2 Corinthians 5:21 ESV**

That is what God's grace is. It is what defines His mercy and love. All that is what defines God's grace and why He extends it. This is a God thing, not a human thing. Only God could do that. Because of His mercy and grace, we can inherit eternal life in heaven with God. Heaven is where He is; there we might be also. **John 14:3**

I think that we often cheapen God's act of grace today, and we frequently belittle God's grace by our desire for things from God more than forgiveness of sin. Remember, God is holy and His mercy and grace must display His holiness as well as His kindness.

Too often we see grace seen as material blessings, financial success and prosperity, and good health and healing blessings. Now, all of these are blessings. They are definitely from God's hand, and they do express the kindness of God, but there are many people who can and are bestowing these things in abundance upon undeserving people. This is a minor and small thing to God. We often expect human government to be the supplier of needs to the disadvantaged and undeserving in life. We call that to be humanitarian in desire.

Yet, the purpose of God's grace goes beyond all that. It is offered not for things, but for forgiveness of sin and to make one acceptable to God to gain entrance to heaven for eternity. Again, God does supply good things to us and things beyond measure to people. He supplies them graciously, just because He loves us. But His major purpose for mercy and grace is for a divine purpose. Mercy and grace is given for forgiveness of sin. Only God can do that. Alexander Pope wrote in his Essay on Criticism, Part 2:

> *"ah, ne'er a thirst of glory boast,*
> *Nor in a critic let man be lost!*
> *Good-nature and good-sense must ever join;*
> *To err is human; to forgive divine."*

Forgiveness is the gracious and merciful act of God to us, and how shall we escape if we neglect such a great and Godly gift, **Hebrews 2:3; John 3:18.** God does Godly things that cannot be duplicated humanly. They can only be humanly received, graciously.

God not only wants us to be forgiven but to grow in grace and love toward others that we meet in life and to offer this same gift of grace to them. We can only do this when we grow in the Lord. What we learn, we give to others so that they may give to others as well.

Have you experienced the mercy and grace of God? You can by admitting that you are a sinner and in need of a Savior. If you would believe that Jesus came to offer forgiveness to you and would repent of your sins, He will forgive you of your sins just because He desires to do so. He will place His righteousness upon you and make you fit for heaven. That is grace, God's grace, and God alone can do that.

Think about it. *Selah!*

### Day 52:  Why Would God Care For Me?

*"When I consider Your heavens, the work of your fingers, The moon and the stars, which you have ordained, What is man that You are mindful of him, And the son of man that you visit him?  For you have made him a little lower than the angels, And You have crowned him with glory and honor."* **Psalm 8:3-5 NKJV**

What is it about mankind, and specifically about me, that would compel a holy God to care, in the least bit, for mankind?  **I John 3:1**   What kind of love does it require for a perfect God to direct all His love to an imperfect and a defective creation?  Why would a faithful God want anything to do with an unfaithful creature?  It takes a God-love, an Agape Love.  It takes an all-knowing God who already knows the conclusion of a matter and has it written down in His journal. *"Let us hear the conclusion of the whole matter: Fear God and keep his commandments, For this is man's all.  For God will bring every work into judgment, Including every secret thing, Whether good or evil."* **Ecclesiastes 12:13-14 NKJV**

In short, God cares and loves you specifically because He chooses to, He wants to, He enjoys your fellowship, and He is faithful, though we might be unfaithful, **Hebrews 10:23; 2 Timothy 2:13.**  God knows all about your failures and shortcomings, and He knew about them before He sent His Son Jesus to earth.  He loves you because you are His creation.  When He created man He said: *". . . it was very good,"* **Genesis 1:31 NKJV.**  But, *"It is not good that man should be alone,"* **Genesis 2:18.**  Because of His great love, God made a compatible helper for man.  He made woman to make him complete.  Men and women need fellowship with each other and with

God in order to be complete. Yes, God also wants fellowship with His handiwork. You are his handiwork: *"For we are his workmanship, created in Christ Jesus for good works, which God prepared beforehand that we should walk in them."* **Ephesians 2:10 NKJV**

God loves and cares for His creation. You are His creation, and He wants to make you a new creation, fit for fellowship with Him for eternity.

Think about it. *Selah!*

# Day 53:  Discernment

*"Oh, the depth of the riches and wisdom and knowledge of God!  How unsearchable are his judgments and how inscrutable his ways!"* **Romans 11:33 ESV**

In making the right decision in our lives, each of us has had moments where we needed great wisdom and knowledge that went beyond ourselves in making a life changing choice.  Those moments where a decision must be made and the choice we make will determine which road we will take.  That choice will affect the quality of life that we will live, and in these moments we need help.  Who do you go to for help?  Where do you turn?  I hope your answer is to our extravagant God.  The extravagant knowledge and wisdom of God cannot be figured out.  But God has the future and us figured out and, therefore, His counsel is great to us.  Though it is impossible for us to understand His decisions and His methods, they can be trusted.

Did you know God wants to help in our big decisions and even in those much smaller ones?  By the way, to God all decisions are small.  We are the ones who give measure to them.  The big decisions in our life are small to God, and those we determine as small are no less than the big ones in our lives.  **James 1:5 NKJV** tells us *"If any of you lacks wisdom, let him ask of God . . . ."*

**Romans 11:33 ESV** defines the quality and depth of God's wisdom, understanding and decision-making: *"Oh, the depth of the riches and wisdom and knowledge of God!  How unsearchable are his judgments and how inscrutable his ways!"* Eugene Peterson in his paraphrase **The Message** says it like this: *"Have you ever come upon anything quite like this extravagant generosity of God, this* *deep, deep wisdom? It's way over our heads. We'll never figure it out."* The **New Living Translation** puts it this way: *"Oh, how great are his riches and wisdom and knowledge! How impossible it is for us to understand his decisions and his ways!"* **Romans 11:33**

The wonder and blessing is that God wants to help us in our decisions. He is there with us in the decision-making, standing close to us, whispering to us: *"And your ears shall hear a word behind you, saying 'This is the way, walk in it.'"* **Isaiah 30:21 ESV**

So, here is the truth:

1. Ask
2. Listen
3. Look
4. Act

Do you have a need for wisdom? Do you need help in discerning what to do and which path to take?

Then, **ask** God for wisdom and **listen and watch** for His voice of knowledge and God-signs of direction. Seek the support of Godly men and women: *"Without counsel, plans go awry, but in the multitude of counselors they are established,"* **Proverbs 15:22 NKJV.** *"Where there is no counsel, the people fall; but in the multitude of counselors there is safety,"* ***Proverbs* 11:14 NKJV.** The Holy Spirit is the teacher and counselor, and He can use Godly men and women to be a visible comfort. So, **Act**, and make the decision.

1. Ask
2. Listen
3. Look
4. Act

Think about it. *Selah!*

## Day 54:  Entertaining Angels Unawares

*"Let brotherly love continue.  Do not neglect to show hospitality to strangers, for thereby some have entertained angels unawares."*  **Hebrews 13:1-2 ESV**

I was on my way home from the church office and anxious to get there because my children were home, and my wife and I had made plans to go out to eat Mexican food.  As I was leaving the city limits of Camilla, Georgia, headed home to Albany, Georgia, I came across a young man hitchhiking. He looked as though he was nineteen or twenty years of age.  He had a backpack and was wearing a sock hat.  I passed him by, which was normal for me, but for some reason, I felt that I needed to give him a ride. I quickly pressed the brake pedal and backed up to him. As I did, he came running toward the car.  "Need a ride?" I asked him.  "Yes," was his reply.  He threw his backpack in the back and sat next to me in the front seat.  He was thin and I noticed his arm was full of tattoos.  "Where are you going?" I enquired.  "Kansas City," he told me.  "Well, you have quite a trip ahead of you don't you?"  He nodded his head.  "My sister lives there and I can be of help to her and find me a job," he said.  "So, you plan on hitchhiking all the way?" I asked.   "Yes," he said, "I just left my mom and dad's house in Cairo, Georgia. They have just come home from Honduras; they are missionaries there."

Many questions invaded my mind, but I felt as though I needed to help him.  I asked, "What is your name?"  He told me it was James.  "Well, James, my name is Danny and I think that the Lord would like for me to buy you a bus ticket to Kansas City."  He quickly responded to my observation, "Oh, no, I'll be okay."  "James," I said, "I have two sons and I wouldn't want them to be out on the road hitchhiking. There are a lot of bad people out there who are looking for an opportunity to take advantage of you." He slumped and I noticed a tear from his eye.

"Well, I know you're thirsty, and hungry, and I'll stop up here to get you some water," I said. I did that, but he only got a bottle of water and some cookies. We got back in my car, and I headed to the bus station to get James a ticket to Kansas City, only to find out that there would not be any buses leaving for Kansas City until the next morning at eight o'clock. "Well, James let's go get you something more substantial to eat," I said. I took James to a local buffet for a meal and then excused myself to make a call on my cell to my wife, Bobbie. "Hey, Bobbie," I said, " I have a bit of a situation here. I know you might not be comfortable with this but I picked up this young man who was hitchhiking to Kansas City. I have promised him that I would buy a bus ticket for him but there will not be any buses leaving until in the morning. So, I'm going to take him to our house to spend the night." There was a brief moment of silence, and then I said, "Go ahead and take the kids and grandchildren to the Mexican restaurant, and I am going to take the young man to Starbucks and then come to eat with you and the family. I will then go back to get him and bring him home to spend the night."

I would have to admit that she was not really totally on board with my plan, but we did it anyway. As I brought James into the house, I introduced him to my family, and we all had a brief time of conversation. Afterwards, I took him to his room and showed him the bathroom and shower.

The next morning before the rest of the family got up, I took James to get breakfast and then to the bus station to purchase the ticket. Everything went well that day and as I waved to James and went back to my car, I found in the seat this note:

"Mr. Danny,

*When I was hungry you fed me, when I was homeless you gave me shelter. When I was without hope you showed me the mercies of the Lord. You are truly a man of God! There is no way I can express how thankful I am. So I will simply say, Thank you!*

*'They will know you by the way you love each other . . . !' You showed me kindness that I haven't seen in a long time. I pray that the Lord will encounter you in ways you've never imagined, that He will bless you and your beautiful family beyond measure. And may He give you all His blessings and great peace of heart and mind.*

*'To you, O Lord, I pray. Don't fail me, Lord, for I am trusting in you. Don't let my enemies succeed. Don't give them victory over me. Show me the path where I should go. O Lord; point out the right road for me to walk. Lead me; teach me; for you are the God who gives me salvation. I have no hope except in You Lord.*
*Amen, and all praise and glory be to him who loved us first.'*
"

Eugene Peterson puts it this way in **The Message**, *"Some have extended hospitality to angels without ever knowing it!"* **Hebrews 13:2 MSG**

I felt as James did when I told him I was going to purchase a bus ticket for him. God had done a great thing for me. This was a God-moment, and I bowed my head in awe of God's presence at that moment to praise Him for His great love to me. I really do believe that this was a moment when I had the privilege of entertaining an angel, and I was totally unaware of it.

How about you? Has there been a time in your life that you have been in the presence of an angel and entertained him for the sole purpose of extending the kindness of God?

*"Or do you presume on the riches of his kindness and forbearance and patience, not knowing that God's kindness is meant to lead you to repentance?"* **Romans 2:4 ESV**

*"But my life is worth nothing to me unless I use it for finishing the work assigned me by the Lord Jesus--the work of telling others the Good News about the wonderful grace of God."* **Acts 20:24 NLT**

Think about it. *Selah!*

## Day 55:  Pray For Your Country

*"And if I announce that I will plant and build up a certain nation or kingdom, but then that nation turns to evil and refuses to obey me, I will not bless it as I said I would."* **Jeremiah 18:9-10 NLT**

*"These United States of America were founded on the Gospel of Jesus Christ,"* said Patrick Henry.  That statement by Patrick Henry is questioned today and I fear for my country.  My desire is that we, as a nation, would return to the values and truths that we once held. How did we get to where we now find ourselves today?

I believe there are two big reasons. One is that the overwhelming majority of Christians don't seem to be concerned about the condition of our country and refuse to admit that our country is in any real danger.  I believe that the majority of Christians in our country today are indifferent and seemingly feel safe as we are and do not see any urgency or need for taking any action.  Therefore, most of us just turn our eyes from what is actually happening.  The second reason is closely related and that is preferred ignorance. Many believers just don't want to know anything beyond what they already know.

If you do not know that you are in danger or you do not see the danger as real danger, then you just sit, look away and do nothing.  Unless we Christians become vigilant in service, watchful, faithful to the cause of Jesus Christ, and pray daily for our nation, our nation will remain on its steady course and become a Godless nation and become a nation of gods.  At that point we will have strayed from Patrick Henry's statement and away from our founding values as a nation: *"These United States of*

*America were founded on the Gospel of Jesus Christ."*

What about you? How do you view our nation? Do you see any real and present danger? Do you pray daily for our nation? Do you vote? Do you support candidates with Biblical world-views? Dr. James David Gray, president of the Southern Baptist Convention in 1951, prayed this prayer at the Sugar Bowl game between Oklahoma and Kentucky.

*"Gracious God:*

*We offer thanks to you today for the blessings that you have showered upon this our beloved land.*

*We thank you for the heritage that we enjoy as Americans. It is our desire that we as a people would be ever mindful of that glorious tradition which is our 'blood-bequeathed' legacy from the past.*

*We also pray today in the critical hour, that we would display the true greatness and spiritual strength of our forefathers and that it would be manifested within us.*

*Grant wisdom to our leaders and courage to all our people that is found only in you alone. Be with those who, are at this moment, bravely fighting for our God given way of life.*

*Put down the forces of evil. Hasten the day when wars shall be no more and righteousness shall cover the earth as the waters cover the sea with forgiveness for our nation and individual sins.*

*We beg it in the name of him who is the Prince of Peace. Amen."*

Perhaps that prayer could not even be publicly proclaimed in our nation today. What happened? How did we get here?

If you want God to bless this nation as He has in the past and protect her as He has in the past, then pray for her and teach your children to have Biblical values and to see that those values are important. Open your eyes and look. What do you see? Then pray this prayer:

> *"God bless America, land that I love,*
> *Stand beside her and guide her,*
> *Through the night, with a light from above."*

> *God bless America, my home sweet home!*
> **Irving Berlin**

Think about it. *Selah!*

### Day 56:  Eye Has Not Seen Nor Ear Heard

*"For since the beginning of the world Men have not heard nor perceived by the ear, Nor has the eye seen any God besides you, Who acts for the one who waits for him. You meet him who rejoices and does righteousness, who remembers you in your ways . . . ."* **Isaiah 64:4-5 NKJV**

Have you ever thought of the might, magnitude and majesty of God?  If after having pondered these things in your mind has it ever puzzled you that God, the one and only God and beside whom there is no other or greater, would desire to do anything for someone like you?  I have often thought of just that and when I do I stand jaw-dropped and speechless in those awesome thoughts.

*"Since the beginning of the world."*  As Isaiah has pinned, the thought of you and me was ever present in this great God's mind.  Why?  I do not think I, nor any other human being, would have the where-with-all to format and arrange the adjectives and nouns to properly relay that type of reasoning.  But God's mind is on you and me.  Wow!

How comforting that thought should be to us.  With this understanding, why should we worry?  With this knowledge, why wouldn't we want to obey His desires since He acts for those of us who wait for Him?  Armed with such knowledge and understanding, why wouldn't we want to inform others of this mighty, majestic, and loving God?  Jesus told us to go tell others about this Good News and be passionate enough to make others into disciples who desire to tell others.  This is the God upon which these United States of America have been founded and that is undeniable, but I fear it is in the process of changing today. I pray that we Christians do our part to just cheerfully and faithfully do good and live in a Godly way. If so, surely our nation would change its dangerous and Godless course.

Why don't you determine to share this thought with someone today? The **New Living Translation** says: *"You welcome those who gladly do good, who follow godly ways,"* **Isaiah 64:5 NLT.** Cheerfully tell someone today.

Think about it. *Selah!*

### Day 57:  My Grace Is Sufficient To The End

*"So to keep me from becoming conceited because of the surpassing greatness of the revelations, a thorn was given me in the flesh, a messenger of Satan to harass me, to keep me from becoming conceited.  Three times I pleaded with the Lord about this, that it should leave me.  But he said to me, 'My grace is sufficient for you, for my power is made perfect in weakness.'  Therefore I will boast all the more gladly of my weaknesses, so that the power of Christ may rest upon me.  For the sake of Christ, then, I am content with weaknesses, insults, hardships, persecutions, and calamities.  For when I am weak, then I am strong."*  **2 Corinthians 12:7-10 ESV**

God's grace is sufficient.  It is sufficient for our everyday need.  God's sufficiency only comes when we have come to the end of our sufficiency.  Have you found God's grace sufficient in your life?  As long as you find yourself not in need of help then you have not experienced God's sufficient hand in your life.  If you have no need in your life, then you have no need for a search for more.

The principle and Biblical truth here is, God provides a daily supply of power needed to do that for which He has called us.  God calls us to do that which we are incapable of doing, and so we need His supply of power.

Paul's purpose for praying was for the removal of a hindrance, a weakness, a thorn in his life.  He was so concerned about this weakness that he fervently prayed about this at three different times.  To Paul, this was a necessary removal but Jesus responded by saying: "<u>Paul, you must serve me in spite of the thorn in your life, in</u>

spite of what you perceive to be a hindrance in your ministry, and in spite of the weakness that has your attention." It was because of the thorn and in the tight grip of this hindrance and this weakness that Paul found the all-sufficient grace of God, which would empower him for victory.

When thorns, hindrances, and weaknesses pop up in our lives, we must know that they are natural and God wants to replace them with supernatural grace. The truth is, we spend too much time and concern focused on weakness and not enough on the God-empowered mission to which we have been called. As long as our mind is focused on the pain, we stop doing that for which God has called us. A friend of mind, Ken Bevel, once said: "Don't exalt your problems, exalt your Lord." God is to be exalted not the pain, thorn, and weakness.

Are you involved in doing what God has called you to do? Are there things that bother you as you do what God has called you to do? What is it that hinders you? May I suggest that you keep your mind off the thorn or distraction in your life and on that which God has called you to do. Place your trust in God, and you will experience joy in the work and in life in general.

"For the sake of Christ, then, I am content with weaknesses, insults, hardships, persecutions, and calamities. For when I am weak, then I am strong." **2 Corinthians 12:7-10 ESV**

Think about it. Selah!

## Day 58: The Ever Present Shepherd

*"Surely goodness and mercy shall follow me all the days of my life; and I will dwell in the house of the Lord forever."*
**Psalm 23:6 KJV**

You can depend upon this fact: If God is leading us and if we are following Him and listening to Him, we will always be with Him. And where God is, Satan flees. **James 4:7**

If God is going – we should follow Him; we should join Him.

If God is providing – we should receive His provisions and not refuse them.

If God is resting - we should rest with Him and we should wait with Him.

Don't fear; have faith.

Don't fret; trust and dwell with Him.

Don't quit; overcome.

Don't look at the problem; look beyond the problem to the Shepherd, the Victor

and the Overcomer. Jesus is our Shepherd, our Victor and our Overcomer.

If we will do these few things, then goodness and mercy shall follow us all the days of our natural lives and forever. Why? Because we are His sheep and we are following the Shepherd.

Think about it. *Selah!*

## Day 59:  Reverential Respect

*". . . He that ruleth over men must be just, ruling in the fear of God. And he shall be as the light of the morning, when the sun riseth, even a morning without clouds; as the tender grass springing out of the earth by clear shining after rain."*
**2 Samuel 23:3-4 KJV**

Eugene Peterson in **The Message** paraphrases this verse as follows: *"Whoever governs fairly and well, who rules in the Fear-of-God, Is like first light at daybreak without a cloud in the sky, Like green grass carpeting earth, glistening under fresh rain."* **2 Samuel 23:3-4 MSG**

Everybody wants justice and fairness but few there are today who seek to govern in the fear of God.  It is the fear of God that brings about justice and fairness.  Justice and fairness give birth to success and lasting happiness.  If the fear of God is not a desire of the one ruling over a people, revolt will soon take place because the people will not have reverence for the ruler.

What does *"fear of God"* mean?   This fear is a reverential respect, an understanding of the power and ability of God and your own limitation of power and ability.  It is when there is a great respect, reverence, and awe of God that peace comes about to those people and the nation.  The fear of God means that you will have no fear for those who would seek to come against you for you are with Him.  This fear means that you will live in an indescribable peace.  This fear of God causes that ruler and people to have full confidence that God is your protection and it is His wrath that will be unleashed upon those you come against.  *"It is a fearful thing to fall into the hands of the living God,"* Hebrews 10:31 ESV tells us.

This is also true in your personal life. When there is a reverential respect for God, it will soon be discovered that as God governs your life and protects your future. It will produce a calm, certain tranquility and complete confidence in the midst of life's turmoil.

Do you have turmoil in your life? Have chords of discord been sounding about your daily life? Look at the next verses that follow David's revelation of a successful leader. The **New Living Translation** puts it this way:

*"Is it not my family God has chosen? Yes, he has made an everlasting covenant with me. His agreement is arranged and guaranteed in every detail. He will ensure my safety and success."* **2 Samuel 23:5 NLT**

With a reverential fear of God also comes a good understanding of life and of eternal life. This is God's peace that is not like this world's peace, which is temporary and only present in this life, but it's a heavenly peace for an eternal future, **John 14:27.** Your success and your safety is eternal, final, and sealed.

So, fear God, serve Him, and be just and gracious to others with a reverential fear of God, and you will bring peace to those around you.

Think about it. *Selah!*

# Day 60: Decisions, Decisions

*"So the LORD must wait for you to come to him so he can show you his love and compassion. For the LORD is a faithful God. Blessed are those who wait for his help."*
**Isaiah 30:18 NLT**

Decision-making is a part of life that will always be with us. We make all types of decisions every day, some may be small and easy in our estimation and others will be great and come with much difficulty. The decision that we make at the moment will shape what we do next, for the better or worse.

Some people seem to be proficient to us in decision-making and others are visibly shaken with the process. Why are decisions difficult and hard? They are difficult because we do not know what will happen next. If we are confident in our self, decision-making comes easy, but it is in those moments of indecision that fretting comes and invades our lives. Where do you place your confidence? If it is in your self, then you will experience fretting and worry when you come to the limit of your efficiency. The only way to avoid fretting and worry in decision-making is to seek a dependable and faithful source. For the believer, that is the guidance of the Holy Spirit, our Comforter and Teacher. Where you place your hope in a decision  then determines if you are comfortable and at peace with the decision.

We read **Isaiah 30:18b & 20-21** in **The Message** as follows: *"God takes the time to do everything right-- everything. Those who wait around for him are the lucky ones . . . . Your teacher will be right there, local and on the job, urging you on whenever you wander left or right: 'This* *is the right road.  Walk down this road.' "*

So, as you live your life in this world, live it in Christ, ask for guidance, and respond to His voice.  Place your faith and hope in his faithfulness and be happy and peaceful.  Decision-making is not easy, but following Christ brings peace in the decision-making.

Think about it.  *Selah!*

## Day 61:  Men Of Prayer, Confident Leaders

*"If my people, which are called by my name, shall humble themselves, and pray, and seek my face, and turn from their wicked ways; then will I hear from heaven, and will forgive their sin, and will heal their land."* **2 Chronicles 7:14 KJV**

It was 1752 that twenty-year-old George Washington carried a personal prayer book, hand-written by his own hand, which he gave the title: *"Daily Sacrifice."* Here is one of those prayers: *"Give me grace to hear thee calling on me in Thy Word, that it may be wisdom, righteousness, reconciliation and peace to the saving of my soul at the day of The Lord.  May I hear it with reverence, receive it with meekness, mingle it with faith that it may be accomplished in me, gracious God, the good work for which thou hast sent it.*

*Bless my family, kindred, friends and country, be our God and guide this day forever for his sake, who lay down in the grave and arose again for us, Jesus Christ, our Lord. Amen."*

In spite of what the media wants us to believe, George Washington was a man of prayer who daily sought for the guiding hand of God.  He acknowledged his need for divine guidance to be the leader *"for the good work which thou has sent it."* I believe this single prayer reveals and gives light to the dependence that our forefathers had upon God in the founding of our great nation.  There have been many great kings, monarchs, and leaders of many lands, but the greatest of them are the ones who loved their people, loved their God, and were great men of prayer.  The great leaders of our great nation were not great because of their strength but great because they were men of great prayer.

*"If my people, which are called by my name, <u>shall humble themselves, and pray, and seek my face, and turn from their wicked ways;</u> then will I hear from heaven, and will forgive their sin, and will heal their land."* **2 Chronicles 7:14 KJV**

Think about it. *Selah!*

## Day 62:  What If God Says No?

*"Three different times I begged the Lord to take it away. Each time he said, 'My grace is all you need.  My power works best in weakness.'  So now I am glad to boast about my weaknesses, so that the power of Christ can work through me."*
**2 Corinthians 12:8-9 NLT**

Jesus told his disciples that they would be able to do greater things than He had done, and He was guaranteeing it to them.  If they needed anything in the work, all they needed to do was to ask for it in prayer to the Father in Jesus' name, and whatever they asked for would be supplied by the Father. **John 14:12 –14**

In **Matthew 21:21-22,** Jesus assured his disciples that as they witnessed Him curse the fruitless fig tree and it died, they would be able to do the same.  If they would pray, have faith, and not doubt, what they prayed for would be done.  He is quoted in **John 15:16** as telling His disciples that He was the one who had chosen them for the ministry.  He wanted them to be fruitful in their ministry, and He wanted their fruit to last so that the Father would give them anything they might ask for using His name.  In **John 14:13,** Jesus says that our request will be answered to glorify the Father in the Son.

God's supply to us is way beyond our wildest dream, as Paul tells us in **Ephesians 3:20** and in **Philippians 4:19.**  Paul assures us that God's supply is given to us according to his riches in heaven through Christ Jesus our Lord.  James tells us in **James 4:2-3** that the reason that we don't have many things is because we haven't asked for them.  We are too busy scheming to get things by our own power. When we do ask, we don't receive because we ask "amiss" by requesting things that we have no right asking for, things that aren't ours to ask for, or we want to have things our own way out of a heart of pride and lust. Also, anything that is out of the will of God and does not honor and glorify God is a selfish request. Things that honor Him and glorify God are those things that are in His perfect will.

Paul emphasizes in **Romans 8:28** that God is actively weaving everything that happens in the lives of those who are the called according to His purpose for their good. God wants only the best for his children just as we want the best for our children, Jesus told his disciples. **Matthew 7:9**

I have asked God for many things that I have not received, and the reason is that I really did not need them or God had something better for me. Sometimes what I asked would have prevented me from representing God well or from being used by Him just as I was, where I was, and without what I had asked for. It's not about me anyway; life is about Him and them. The Great Commission is "Go ye therefore" and the Great Commandment is to love others as God loves me. God's desire is to use me to help someone else who is in need of salvation or His love through me. Sometimes I was used as the answer to the prayer of someone else, and I was the object of God's good hand upon another.

When I pray, I ask and often continue to ask until I know that what I have been asking is not what God would have for me or that He has something better for me. Do you remember what Jesus prayed in the Garden: *"Father, if you are willing, please take this cup of suffering away from me. Yet, I want your will to be done, not mine,"* **Luke 22:42 NLT.** The cup was God's will for Him. Sometimes we want to do things in the wrong way. When Jesus was arrested in the Garden, the disciples came to His defense and He told his disciples to put away their swords; that wasn't his plan. If He needed help, He had at his disposal 12 legions of angels if He wanted them, but even that was not God's will for Him, **Matthew 26:53.** The Father's will was for Jesus to die for our sins.

Here is the bottom line: Sometimes God's answer to us is yes, at other times the answer is no, and then there are times His answer to us is, "Wait a minute; it is not the right time now." What we must do at all times is to trust His loving heart, knowing His goodness is greater than our request. What I am saying is to be happy with a "no" or a "not now." Neither means that He doesn't hear us or doesn't love us.

Prayer is not a means for us to get our will done in heaven, as we want to have it done on earth. Sometimes God's loving response to us is "no" or "not now."

Think about it. *Selah!*

## Day 63: There Is Nothing God Cannot Do

*"For nothing will impossible with God."* **Luke 1:37 ESV**

Has God provided all that you needed in the past? Is He providing all that you need right now? If He has provided for your need in the past and He is providing your need right now, then you can confidently trust Him to supply all that you will need in your near future, far future and eternal future.

In **Hebrews 13:8-9 NLT** we find, *"Jesus Christ is the same yesterday, today, and forever. . . . Your strength comes from God's grace."* God supplies your needs and then goes far beyond your need. He supplies exceedingly abundantly above anything that you could even dream about. God supplies us with blessings that are undeserved and reflect His favor to us. Why? He does this "just because," because He wants to do it. There is no other reason, "just because."

He wants to bless us because He is loving and kind. It's God's love that springs blessing into action. God is love but love is not God. Love is not a god; it is the character of God. There are some elements in life that we define as love, but those are selfish, restrained, undependable and shallow. God's love is Agape love, an undeserved love; therefore, it is without end and is not dependent on anything but Him. His love is sustained, strong, fulfilling, dependable, genuine, and pure. It builds us up, encourages us, and brings joy to our lives. God's love is beyond measure and indescribable. In God's love for you, there was no time that He did not know all there is to know about you. There is nothing about you that was unknown to Him, even before the foundations of the world. Before you were born He knew you and all that you would do from the time you were conceived until the time you would die on this earth. Knowing all of this, He wrote everything down in His book, Psalm **139:16.** Therefore, you cannot surprise God by what you do. He already knew it. There was never a time He did not know it and he died for you anyway. This is the God who is the same yesterday, today, and forever. This is the God who wants to supply all your needs and wants to love you. So, why are you fretting over life? Why are you worried? Where is your faith? Why don't you just do your best and give God the rest?

You are only causing yourself harm by worrying and doubting that God will do what He has said that He would do. He knows you and your need and has made provisions to meet all your need, so watch him do it.

Think about it. *Selah!*

## Day 64: Forgiven?

*"You were dead because of your sins and because your sinful nature was not yet cut away. Then God made you alive with Christ, for he forgave all our sins. He canceled the record of the charges against us and took it away by nailing it to the cross. In this way, he disarmed the spiritual rulers and authorities. He shamed them publicly by his victory over them on the cross."*
**Colossians 2:13 – 15 NLT**

Forgiven? Yes, God has if you have accepted His offer of forgiveness. It is divinely legal and totally trustworthy. It is as real as the cross of Christ. You are the only missing factor in forgiveness. If you have not accepted Christ Jesus as your Lord and Savior, He stands patiently before you with His gift of forgiveness, just waiting for you to freely take it. It's your move, your call.

Forgiveness is freely offered and is freely taken, but it was not without cost. Forgiveness came by the death of Christ on the cross and was confirmed by His resurrection from the grave. **Colossians 2:15 NLT** states *" . . . He shamed them publicly by his victory over them on the cross."* Therefore, as we stand before Christ at the Judgment Seat of Christ, we stand righteous, clean, pure and free of sin. We have the righteousness of Christ upon us, **2 Corinthians 5:21.**

**Hebrews 4:13 ESV** says: *"And no creature is hidden from his sight, but all are naked and exposed to the eyes of him to whom we must give account."* The believer stands in the righteousness of Christ, FORGIVEN!

Since God has forgiven you of your sin and Jesus has died for the forgiveness of your sin, can't you forgive yourself of your sin?

Think about it. *Selah!*

# Day 65: Persecution

*"Here is a call for the endurance of the saints, those who keep the commandments of God and their faith in Jesus."* **Revelation 14:12 ESV**

Pain produces strength. Athletes put themselves through painful exercise and conditioning to make themselves strong. Students put themselves through stressful study to gain knowledge and wisdom to receive a degree or diploma. Solders must place themselves through insults, painful training and be deprived of all types of freedoms to shape themselves into a fighting machine that will stand up against the enemy who goes through the same conditioning and training to overcome them.

In the same manner the Christian must suffer persecution. Persecution produces strength and endurance. Amos the prophet wrote in **Amos 6:1 KJV,** *"Woe, to them that are at ease in Zion. . . ."* **The New Living Translation** puts it this way: *"What sorrow awaits you who lounge in luxury in Jerusalem. . . ."* "A body in motion, stays in motion, a body at rest, stays at rest," the law of physics proclaims.

Persecution is to be expected. Jesus prepared his disciples for persecution by telling them that the world would suffer persecution and not to be surprised by it, **John 16:1-6.** Today, believers all throughout the world are suffering persecution and great persecution because of their faith. The believers in America are at ease, but I am afraid it will not be for long. We think we are above persecution. We are at rest, and so we stay at rest. Jesus has told us to be in motion, to go and make disciples, and we have not.

Have you suffered persecution? You will. *"Here is a call for the endurance of the saints, those who keep the commandments of God and their faith in Jesus."* **Revelation 14:12 ESV**

Think about it. *Selah!*

## Day 66:  Things May Not Be As They Appear

*". . . I have uttered what I did not understand, things too wonderful for me, which I did not know."* **Job 42:3 ESV**

Do you remember the famous magician David Copperfield doing disappearing feats on television? Remember the time he made Diamond Head and the Statue of Liberty disappear? Well, they may have seemed to disappear, but they did not, it was only a clever trick. Some times things are not as they appear to be.  The adage is: *"Don't believe anything you hear and only half of what you see."*  To a large degree that is true.

Job is recorded to say in **Job 10:3 ESV,** *"Does it seem good to you to oppress, to despise the work of your hands and favor the designs of the wicked?"*  God had not rejected Job.  He was proving him before Satan, *". . . there is none like him on the earth, a blameless and upright man, who fears God and turns away from evil."* **Job 1:8 ESV**

Everyone misjudged the event. Everyone thought they were witnessing the judgment of God on Job, but in truth it was the hand of Satan upon Job seeking to devour him while the hand of God was on Job, sustaining him in the midst of great tribulation.  Job was actually God's prized jewel.

Job finally concludes that he was talking out of his head, trying to explain things that he knew nothing about.  Remember, God is good and His good hand is upon His good people.  We are the work of His hand and from His hand we receive all and more than we need.  We must have the faith to endure tribulation.  Jesus told us that in the world we would have tribulation.  He said that the world hated Him and they would also hate us just because we love Him. **John 16:33 & 15:18-20**

Are things mounting up on you now? Well, take heart. God is with you, and the Holy Spirit is beside you whispering the wisdom that you need. You know, "this world is not our home, we're just a passing through," as the old Gospel song reminds us. Heaven is our home, and we are on the journey going there. The journey is long and hard, but it is well worth the effort of the going. It may seem that God is not with us but He is with us and will never forsake us, not even for a moment. Don't go by what you see and hear in the world. Hold to what God has said. You can trust Him. Yes, you are going to make it through all this "stuff." You are God's jewel!

Think about it. *Selah!*

## Day 67: Commitment, Contentment, Happiness, and Joy

*"And whatsoever you do in word or deed, do all in the name of the Lord Jesus, giving thanks to God and the Father by him."* **Colossians 3:17 KJV**

Everyone wants to be happy and joy is what produces happiness. Are you happy? Where is your joy? Has your joy and happiness taken a hike for the moment? If not, it often does if we allow it. To be happy and joyful, one must be contented and committed to happiness and joy. We must learn to be contented by being committed. The apostle Paul wrote in **Philippians 4:11 KJV,** *"Not that I speak in respect of want: for I have learned, in whatsoever state I am, therewith to be content."* Paul did what he did for the glory of Christ Jesus, and he was happy with the results of what he did.

John Wesley wrote:

"I am no longer my own, but yours.
Put me to what you will, rank me with whom you will.
Put me to doing, put me to suffering.
Let me be employed for you or laid aside for you.
Exalted for you or brought low for you.

Let me be full, let me be empty.
Let me have all things, let me have nothing.
I freely and heartily yield all things to your pleasure and disposal.

And know, O glorious and blessed God, Father, Son and Holy Spirit,
You are mine, and I am thine.

So be it.
And the covenant, which I have made on earth,
Let it be ratified in heaven.
Amen"

It takes commitment to something to be happy and a greater determination to be happy where you are for the glory of God.  The Psalmist David wrote in **Psalm 16:11 KJV,** *". . . in thy presence is fullness of joy . . . ."*

If you are committed to God and in the presence of God, then you have joy and happiness, and you are contented.

Think about it. *Selah!*

## Day 68: Are You Whipped or Whipped?

*"Wherefore I remind you to stir up the gift of God which is in you through the laying on of my hands. For God has not given us a spirit of fear, but of power and of love and of a sound mind."* **2 Timothy 1:6-7 NKJV**

As the waitress brings a slice of cherry pie to her customer in the commercial seen on TV, she asks the question: *Oil or cream?* The Coca-Cola jingle states: *"It's the real thing, that's the way that it is, Coca-Cola is Coke!"* Do you want the real stuff or a substitute? The obvious answer is: We desire the real stuff. Jesus is the Truth, the real thing, and beside Him there is no other. All else is merely a substitute, a facsimile. In **2 Timothy 1:6,** Paul encourages Timothy to stir up, to whip up or to fan into a flame, that real and original gift that was given him and was still in him.

God has given each of us a special gift and that gift must be continually stirred, whipped, and fanned to keep it real and effective. To often, it seems, we are inclined to do a different "whipping-up;" we want to beat up on ourselves or whip-up on others when things get difficult. This "whipping" is a discouragement and is of no benefit. Never allow yourself or another fellow believer to be a discourager. We are tempted to let it simmer or allow it to grow cold and soon let it go, or just give up.

Determine to be an encourager to others, don't whip-up, or "beat up," yourself or others. "Stir-up" your brothers and sisters and be around others who will help you to stir up the gift that is within you. Have you been "whipped" or are you "whipped-up?"

Think about it. *Selah!*

## Day 69: Don't Exalt Your Problem, Exalt The Lord

*"Yet even now, be free from your captivity! Leave Babylon and the Babylonians. Sing out this message! Shout it to the ends of the earth! The Lord has redeemed his servants, the people of Israel."* **Isaiah 48:20 NLT**

Ken Bevel is the Pastor of Connections and Events at Sherwood Baptist Church in Albany, Georgia, where my wife and I are members. He is a man of compassion with a big smile and a heart to match. He said in a service: *"Don't exalt your problems, exalt The Lord!"* I really like that, don't you?

Too often we allow our difficulties and the troubles of life to rob us of the joy of our life in Christ Jesus. Jesus has set us free from the penalty of sin and given us eternal life through Him. For that we should be singing a loud song of praise and exaltation to our great Redeemer and exalt him with our voice of singing!

In **Isaiah 48:20** Isaiah encourages the Israeli nation to *"Shout it to the ends of the earth! The Lord has redeemed his servants, the people of Israel."* I think we miss a great deal of celebration because we exalt our problems rather than our great Redeemer. While we should be singing and shouting for joy in celebration of our redemption, it seems we tend to give undo credibility to the trouble that is around us, and thus live in unnecessary sadness.

Refuse to be sad and cast down in your life. Leave your captivity with all its trouble, sing and exult with the sound of victory to our great Redeemer, and God's joy will fill your life.

Think about it. *Selah!*

# Day 70: Excellence

*"Now to Him who is able to do exceedingly abundantly above all . . ."*
**Ephesians 3:20 NKJV**

To excel is to go beyond the norm, above the great, and into that which can only be imagined. Excelling is going beyond what you by yourself are incapable of doing. My wife, Bobbie, is a great lover of music and a much greater and efficient musician than I. It wasn't until after we were married that I began to excel as a Minister of Music. She made me better than I was capable of being on my own. She was the good hand of God upon me helping to mold me into the musician I came to be. But God takes us even further, exceedingly abundantly above all that we could even dream about and into His capabilities.

Oswald Chambers has said: *"All efforts of worth and excellence are difficult. The Christian life is gloriously difficult, but its difficulty does not make us faint and cave in--it stirs us up to overcome."* Excelling takes effort. It includes pain and involves others partnering with you to get you beyond yourself and others. Strive to be around those who are better than you are. If you are the best around you, you will never improve. Iron sharpens iron. Never be intimidated by those who are better than you are. Use them to make improvements in your life.

No one strives to be average. The music ministry of the church that I attend is excellent. I was motivated to become part of that ministry precisely because of the excellence that is obvious weekly. If my observation of that ministry was: *"Wow! Did you hear that! I mean, that was average! That was a solid "C" for sure! Are you thinking what I'm thinking? Yeah, I want to be part of that!"* Well, that was ridiculous, because *average* is just not a draw at all, is it? No one notices *average* or is changed by *average*.

Excelling requires a stirring up and adding to. Paul tells Timothy to *". . . Stir up the gift of God which is in you . . . ."* **2 Timothy 1:6**

Don't be satisfied with something that is easily achieved or try to be like someone else. Strive and press on toward the mark of God, the prize. When you strive for excellence, you will draw others and inspire others to join you. Also, don't be cast down or discouraged by your effort to excel for Christ because you have little help. There are few who excel and that is why you are admired. You are above everyone else. Jesus Christ is worth the effort. Keep your eyes upon Him and press on to the Excellency of Christ. *"Yet indeed I also count all things loss for the excellence of the knowledge of Christ Jesus my Lord, for whom I have suffered the loss of all things, and count them as rubbish, that I may gain Christ."* **Philippians 3:8 NKJV**

Think about it. *Selah!*

# Day 71: Your Gift From God

*"For this reason I remind you to fan into flame the gift of God, which is in you through the laying on of my hands, for God gave us a spirit not of fear but of power and love and self-control"* **2 Timothy 1:6 ESV**

Everyone enjoys getting a gift.  For birthdays, Christmas, anniversaries, and all types of parties for various special occasions, we give and receive gifts from friends, family, and loved ones.  We remember them with fondness, and a smile upon our face.  Gifts are expressions of love and appreciation.  They are presented with joy and with eager anticipation by the giver.  Gifts carry with them feelings of encouragement for the receiver and pride for the giver.

God has a special gift for each believer and that gift came with divine thought and consideration.  It is not a practical gift, but one that is lavishly soaked with love and luxuriously sought out with you in mind.  It is an expensive gift and an unexpected gift offered with love.  It is given to be a blessing and to bring about a feeling of worth to the receiver.  The gift has "you" written all over it and glorifies the giver, God Himself.

Paul reminds Timothy about when he thought about him.  He remembered Timothy's gift and he remembered their time together.  He remembered Timothy's mother and grandmother and the home in which Timothy was raised.  He remembered the training that his mother and grandmother gave him.  He remembered the heritage that he had and the great faith that was evidenced in Timothy's life. Because of all of this, he reminds Timothy: *"For this reason I remind you to fan into flame the gift of*

*God, which is in you through the laying on of my hands, for God gave us a spirit not of fear but of power and love and self-control"* **2 Timothy 1:6 ESV.**

Sometimes we need to be reminded of the gift that we have been given and the joy that was associated with that gift. When we do, it gives us added determination to carry on in spite of the trouble we may be experiencing in our present life. We remember how God worked in our lives in the past, and it gives us great hope for the future. We are reminded of the power that we have in God that is ours, and we must use self-control or take personal initiative to press on, to stir up and fan the flame of power again, and to take courage and do.

If we want to look back, remember the power not the trouble. Remember the victory not the opposition. Remember the gift and the giver. So, I encourage you to fan the flame of your great gift that was given to you and to use it.

Think about it. *Selah!*

## Day 72: So, Where Are You Now?

*"Only let each person lead the life that the Lord has assigned to him, and to which God has called him. This is my rule in all the churches."* **1 Corinthians 7:17 ESV**

Wishing you were somewhere else is a very common desire. The adage is: "The grass is greener on the other side of the fence." It always seems as though the other person has it better than we have. Discontentment is something that prevents many from reaching the height they could were it not for them dwelling on their disadvantages. If you want to be successful in anything, you must put your whole being toward that goal.

Many a home has been broken up because of the discontentment of people who have their eyes focused on others rather than what they have. The Christian life and even the church itself often falls short of its goal and aim due to the lure of discontentment and skepticism of their place. Paul addresses this cancer: *"Only let each person lead the life that the Lord has assigned to him, and to which God has called him. This is my rule in all the churches."* **1 Corinthians 7:17 ESV**

Accept your lot in life, accept the condition in which you find yourself, and accept your place. Eugene Peterson puts it this way in **The Message**: *"And don't be wishing you were someplace else or with someone else. Where you are right now is God's place for you. Live and obey and love and believe right there"* **1 Corinthians 7:17.**

The coveting and lusting for other things and positions is a sin. Take your eyes off those things and positions and be faithful where you are.  As you allow God to use you, then you will experience something that is way beyond your wildest dream and much more than you would have ever imagined.  Where you are is where God has led you and where He has sustained you, blessed you, and allowed you to bless others.

There is an old Gospel hymn written by Ira D. Ogdon with the title: *Brighten the Corner Where You Are.*  The last verse reads:

*"Here for all your talent you may surely find a need,*
*Here reflect the Bright and Morning Star,*
*Even from your humble hand the bread of life may feed*
*Brighten the corner where you are".*

*"Only let each person lead the life that the Lord has assigned to him, and to which God has called him. This is my rule in all the churches."*  **1 Corinthians 7:17 ESV**

Think about it.  *Selah!*

# Day 73: A Friend

*"A friend loves at all times . . ."* **Proverbs 17:17 ESV**

They say you can count all your real friends on one hand and in most cases that is true. What does it take to be a friend and make a friend? It takes putting into action spiritual gifts and exercising the Fruits of the Spirit.

Notice what Paul wrote in **Romans 12:**

*"Let love be genuine. Abhor what is evil; hold fast to what is good. Love one another with brotherly affection. Outdo one another in showing honor. . . . Rejoice in hope, be patient in tribulation, be constant in prayer. Contribute to the needs of the saints and seek to show hospitality. Bless those who persecute you; bless and do not curse them. Rejoice with those who rejoice, weep with those who weep. Live in harmony with one another. Do not be haughty, but associate with the lowly. Never be wise in your own sight."* **Romans 12:9-10; 12-16 ESV**

Here are the truths for friendship:

- Be honest, trustworthy and confidential.
- Be humble, approachable, and comfortable around others.
- Be available, usable, and at hand.
- Be dependable, consistent, and faithful.
- Be real, not a pretender
- Be teachable
- Be a resource, a very present help.

Who do you call in time of need? Who calls you in time of need?

Think about it. *Selah!*

### Day 74: Together As One

*"The human body has many parts, but the many parts make up one whole body. So it is with the body of Christ."*
**1 Corinthians 12:12 NLT**

Church, we are family! A family works together, laughs together, cries together, looks out for each other, and loves each other. A family brings about confidence in times of difficulty. It is supportive in the effort to bring about good to the others, the wellbeing of the others, and a secure future. A family should know its history and should have a solid understanding of where it is today. It should strive for excellence and not be satisfied with the easy way as it focuses on the future.

The family should recognize the gifts and various skills that each individual member has which can make for a better life. I used to jokingly remark to others that I didn't know everything but what I didn't know my brother Dave knew and so when we were together we knew everything. We do need each other to obtain excellence. I cannot excel without the skills of others and they cannot excel without me; and none of us can achieve the divine goal that God has for us outside the mighty hand of God.

We are one body united in Christ Jesus. **1 Corinthians 12:12**

We need to be more than we can be by coming together with the wisdom, knowledge, skills, and strengths of others. Together with the hand of God, we can be what He would have us to be. Are you going through life alone or with others?

Think about it. *Selah!*

# Day 75:  Second Fiddle

*"Love from the center of who you are; don't fake it.  Run for dear life from evil; hold on for dear life to good.  Be good friends who love deeply; practice playing second fiddle."*
**Romans 12:9-10 MSG**

The New King James Version says: *"Be kindly affectionate to one another with brotherly love, in honor giving preference to one another;"* **Romans 12:10 NKJV.** This *"giving preference to one another"* is the idea of seeking to play second fiddle.  Second fiddle is a substitute to someone considered superior to you. Playing second fiddle is playing without recognition. Second fiddle is not a position that anyone would naturally seek to reach.  Second fiddle has no glory, yet Paul tells believers that they should practice playing second fiddle.  Seeking recognition should not be the reason that we do things for Christ.  We should do things for Christ so that He may have the glory, not ourselves.

Not only should Christ get the glory but also our life should be a reflector of the light of Christ to all who may be watching us.  We should display the light, the Good News, and the love of God as Jesus commanded us.  It is the reason we are on this earth.

Paul writes in **Romans 2:4** that the kindness of God leads to repentance. Believers should desire to display that kindness and love through our living and our fellowship together.  Bible commentator Donald Grey Barnhouse in his commentary on Romans writes: *"Christian fellowship is not based on the amount of creedal knowledge that various people have in their heads but in the outgoing life of Christ that they have in their hearts.*

*Christian fellowship is not a matter of light but of life."*

Jesus told his disciples that people would recognize them as followers of Him and as believers by the love that they have for each other. Love is the key element of the life in Christ. God is love, but love is not God. Love is a reflection of the glory of God. Love is the new commandment that Jesus gave His disciples, **John 13:34; 15:12.**
If your ambition is to reach a level of leadership, it is the wrong ambition. Your ambition should be to be a servant, to play second fiddle, and wait for Christ to put you in first chair when He desires. That would be His doing and not yours.

Does it bother you to play second fiddle?

Think about it. *Selah!*

## Day 76:  Two Categories Of Sin

*"For all have sinned, and come short of the glory of God;"*
**Romans 3:23  KJV**

We are all sinners when we are born into this world. We read in **Romans 5:12:** *"You know the story of how Adam landed us in the dilemma we're in – first sin, then death, and no one exempt from either sin or death"* **The Message**.    So, mankind is not basically good, he is basically bad or sinful.

Paul continues this thought of sin in **Romans 5:18-19** by saying: *"Here it is in a nutshell:  Just as one person* (Adam) *did it wrong and got us in all this trouble with sin and death, another person* (Jesus Christ) *did it right and got us out of it. But more than just getting us out of trouble, he got us into life!  One man said no to God and put many people in the wrong; one man said yes to God and put many in the right"* **The Message**.

Augustine commented in his, **Handbook on Faith, Hope, and Love:**

*"We sin from two causes: either from not seeing what we ought to do, or else from not doing what we have already seen we ought to do.  Of these two, the first is ignorance of evil; the second, weakness.*

*We must surely fight against both; but we shall surely be defeated unless we are divinely helped, not only to see what we ought to do, but also, as sound judgment increased, to make our love of righteousness victor over our love of those things because of which – either by desiring to possess them or by fearing to lose them – we fall opened eyed, into sin. In this latter case, we are not only sinners – which we are even when we sin through ignorance – but also lawbreakers: for we do not do what we should , and we do what we know already we should not."*

**James 4:17 ESV** tells us: *"So whoever knows the right thing to do and fails to do it, for him it is sin."* Sin is natural but God's forgiveness is sure and complete. When we take Jesus Christ as our Savior, the righteousness of Jesus takes away and disposes of all our sin.

We are going to sin because we are sinful creatures living in a sinful world. God's forgiveness cleanses known and unknown sin, sins that we commit by doing and sins that we commit by not doing.

Have you come to the point in your life that you realize that you are a sinful person in need of a Savior? Jesus is standing before you right now and wants to solve that problem, so why not admit to Him that you are a sinner, and acknowledge Him to be the only begotten Son of God and Savior of the world. Take Him as your Savior now and He will take your sin and give you His righteousness in exchange. By doing this, your life is now in His hands and your eternal future will be with Him in heaven.

You may be a believer but are not doing what you know that you should do. Perhaps you are making all types of excuses but you know those excuses are invalid. Release them to Jesus and take His hand to lead you out of the clutches of that sin. Give the Holy Spirit free reign in your life. By doing this, your life will be much happier, and you will soon see God doing mighty things in your life that you could not have ever dreamed.

Ask for forgiveness and pray for guidance away from sin. God is our light and our salvation. He is our light to see sin and our salvation to overcome our weakness to sin.

Think about it. *Selah!*

## Day 77: An Example To Others

*"Here's a word you can take to heart and depend on: Jesus Christ came into the world to save sinners. I'm proof – Public Sinner Number One – of someone who could never have made it apart from sheer mercy. And now he shows me off – evidence of his endless patience – to those who are right on the edge of trusting him forever. Deep honor and bright glory to the King of All Time – One God, Immortal, Invisible, ever and always. Oh yes!"* **1 Timothy 1:15-17 MSG**

Paul calls himself the chief of sinners or as Eugene Peterson paraphrases it in **The Message**, *"Public Sinner Number One,"* **1 Timothy 1:15**. I don't think that Paul was overstating the point or being humble. He **was** the chief of sinners. That is why he can say that he was used as an example of the extent of the forgiveness and the *"evidence of his endless patience – to those who are right on the edge of trusting him forever,"* **1 Timothy 1:16 MSG**.

Think of it, the blood of Jesus Christ is more than sufficient to cleanse us by Christ Jesus and His righteousness. If everyone were to take the offer of God's forgiveness, the righteousness of Jesus was more than enough to cover all the sins ever committed by the people of this world for all time, **Romans 5:20.**

This means, that all the worst of the worst people in the whole history of the world past and until the concluding day of time could have the righteousness of Jesus as payment in full for all their sins. *"For He* (God the Father) *made Him* (Jesus the Son) *who knew no sin to be sin for us* (whosoever believes in Him), *that we* (those who believe in the Son) *might become the righteousness of God in Him"* (the Son, Jesus) **2 Corinthians 5:21 NKJV.**

Is that not the most wonderful, though unthinkable, act of love that could be thought? Now that is a God thing, for sure! With this understanding, if God would want to forgive Paul, the chief of sinners, certainly He would want to forgive you of your sin. By receiving His gift of forgiveness, you then become as pure as Jesus because you have His righteousness upon you. Why, you might ask? God's love for you requires it, and His desire to have fellowship with you inspires it.

Now, if He wants to give you such a marvelous and costly gift, how unloving, unthankful, hateful, and unthinkable it is to reject His gift. Jesus tells Nicodemus in **John 3:17–18 ESV:** *"For God did not send his Son into the world to condemn the world, but in order that the world might be saved through him. Whoever believes in him is not condemned, but whoever does not believe is condemned already, because he has not believed in the name of the only Son of God."*

God's desire is for you to spend eternity with Him in heaven rather than spend eternity in hell with Satan, His angels, and all those who have and will reject Him. Hell was not created for you. It was created for Satan and his angels, **Matthew 25:41,** so if you reject His free gift, you go as an intruder to the place where Satan is. Jesus came to give you an option, **John 3:18.**

You might say that what I have just written is merely my thoughts or a myth. Well, for the sake of argument, let's say you are right. Am I worse off after I die believing this? No, I am not. But suppose I am right, will you be worse off after you die? Yes, you will be.

*"For God so loved the world that he gave . . ."* **John 3:16 KJV**. Will you receive?

Think about it. *Selah!*

## Day 78: Do People Put You Down?

*". . . count yourselves blessed every time people put you down or throw you out or speak lies about you to discredit me. What it means is that the truth is too close for comfort and they are uncomfortable. You can be glad when that happens – give a cheer, even! – for though they don't like it. I do! And all heaven applauds. And know that you are in good company. My prophets and witnesses have always gotten into this kind of trouble."* **Matthew 5:11-12 MSG**

From childhood we all have had to deal with others saying things about us that were not true. It seems as though people get "a high" from telling and spreading something slanderous and unfounded about another. That bothers everyone when that happens. Most likely, you have been involved in saying something bad about someone such as a politician, a neighbor, or maybe even a friend. All of that is wrong. We may have thought that the tasty bit of information was true, but later found out that it was not. We felt bad, but the rumor and gossip had already been uttered. We placed our credibility upon on it, and it was tarnished when we stated it.

Thomas A' Kempis writes in <u>The Imitation of Christ</u>: *"Shun the gossip of men as much as possible, for discussion of worldly affairs, even thought sincere, is a great distraction inasmuch as we are quickly ensnared and captivated by vanity. Many a time I wish that I had held my peace and had not associated with men. Why, indeed do we converse and gossip among ourselves when we so seldom part without a troubled conscience?"*

In the Sermon on the Mount Jesus taught: *"Bless are you when others revile you and persecute you and utter all kinds of evil against you falsely on my account. Rejoice and be glad, for your reward is great in heaven . . .* " **Matthew 5:11-12**. The thing to keep in mind is people are gifted in saying evil but Jesus is faithful to reward you for the temporary discomfort of gossip against you.

It was the religious community at the time of Jesus that spread the lies and sought to kill Him because of who He was. They wanted to silence Him, put Him down, and do away with Him because He spoke the truth. Jesus was the Truth, He was the true Light, and He was and still is the Son of God.

Jesus told His disciples that the world hated Him and that they would also hate them because they were His followers. He concluded this statement with the encouraging words: "So, don't worry about the talk; I have overcome the talkers," **John 16:33.** In this case, it is what you know as well as who you know that counts. You know the Victor, the King, the very Son of God. His thoughts about you are all that matters in the end of the world and throughout eternity. When the world puts you down, remember Jesus is going to take you up.

May I ask you a question now? What do you think about Christ, who is He?

Think about it. *Selah!*

## Day 79: The Lone Ranger Was No Loner

*"Then the Lord God said, 'It is not good that the man should be alone; I will make him a helper fit for him.' "*
**Genesis 2:18 ESV**

No one needs to be by himself all the time. Even the Lone Ranger had Tonto. He may have been the last of the Texas Rangers at the time, but he had a friend. Mankind is made for fellowship, fellowship with God first and then fellowship with others. We need both. Without fellowship and by ostracizing himself, a person is not able to reach the height that he could achieve. The word *ostracize* is a good word, a very descriptive word, to use here in that the ostrich has the reputation of placing his head in the sand when danger may be lurking. It is a flightless bird that can take fight from danger by running 31 miles per hour, but sometimes it will hide its head to bring about false safety.

When we ostracize ourselves we, too, create a since of false security; yet, we are actually creating a greater chance of danger and failure. We need each other. We need fellowship. A professor of mine at Detroit Bible College, Dr. William BeVier, defined the word *"fellowship"* in **Philippians 1:5** as "two fellows in a ship."

When God created man, he created him for fellowship. In **Genesis 2:18** we read that God said: *"It is not good that the man should be alone;"* so He made a helper, a companion for him. When Adam and Eve hid from God after they sinned by disobeying God, their hiding did not make the matter better. It just added to the matter.

Too often we continue to hide and remove ourselves from situations that seem to be, and perhaps may be, unsolvable at the moment. But, that is the time we need to seek others to help solve what we are unable to solve alone. The Lone Ranger was a good shot and had a fast horse and great training, but he needed Tonto. We need the help and wisdom of God and those whom He has placed in our lives to bring about a solution and be a present help with the load.

In **Exodus 18** we are told about a visitor Moses had, Jethro his father-in-law, who witnessed Moses being caught up in a situation that would soon bring him down. Though Moses was trying to solve the problems of millions of people, he was trying to do it alone. Jethro told Moses: *"What you are doing is not good. You and the people with you will certainly wear yourselves out, for the thing is too heavy for you. You are not able to do it alone."* **Exodus 18:17-18 ESV**

Moses was unable to see the situation that he had allowed to come about, one that would soon wear him and the people out. The people had problems but they had to take a number and wait. Moses' problem was that he was being stressed and didn't know it. The people were stressed by having to wait for a solution to their problem.

There are many examples of good people isolating themselves when problems pop up. Elijah hid himself, **1 Kings 18**, and that event came on the heels of a great victory and display of God's power.

**Proverbs 18:1 ESV** *"Whoever isolates himself seeks his own desire, he breaks out against all sound judgment."* Isolation is not the answer. God's Word is the answer and others are his weapons to use in the battle.

Think about it. *Selah!*

## Day 80: The Warriors

*"For every boot of the tramping warrior in battle tumult and every garment rolled in blood will be burned as fuel for the fire.* **Isaiah 9:5 ESV**

What does a warrior look like? E. B. Sledge in his book, **With The Old Bread,** which was an eye witness account of his Marine buddies' fight in the Pacific Theater of World War 2, described a fighting warrior: *"The infantryman's calloused hands were nearly blackened by weeks of accumulation of rifle oil, mosquito repellant (an oily liquid called Skat), dirt, dust, and general filth. Overall he was stooped and bent by general fatigue and excessive physical exertion. If approached closely enough for conversation, he smelled bad."*

Warriors have upon them the smell and the look of victory. The smell and look of victory is generally odious to those who do not know war or battle. But it is the warrior who secures the freedom and ease of those who do not know war and often protest war and the warrior.

The warriors for the cause of Christ are described in **Hebrews 11:37-38 ESV:** *"They were stoned, they were sawn in two, they were killed with the sword. They went about in skins of sheep and goats, destitute, afflicted, mistreated – of whom the world was not worthy – wandering about in deserts and mountains, and in dens and caves of the earth."*

Yet, the smell of victory brings about the *". . the aroma of Christ to God among those who are being saved and among those who are perishing,"* **2 Corinthians 2:15 ESV.** We are in a battle not against people, flesh, and blood but principalities and powers, and workers of iniquity in heavenly places, **Ephesians 6:12.** We, too, must put on the armor of God for this fight. The fight will not be a quick one but a lifelong one, a smelly one, a dirty one; yet, though difficult, it is not beyond our source of power, equipment, and supply. We must do these two things: stand in the battle and as we stand, we must trust our armor .

Are you a warrior?

Think about it. *Selah!*

### Day 81: You Are Not Being Pushed Around, You Are Being Positioned

*". . . according to the power at work within us."*
**Ephesians 3:20b ESV**

No one wants to be pushed around, bullied, or taken advantage of. Our first inclination is to resist and push back when those moments come. The truth is, being pushed around is a natural trait of humanity. To push around is a way of having one's own way. God wants us to allow Him to have His way in us, but He does not accomplish His way by forcing us to move. He asks us to move, He gives us the opportunity to move and thereby do His will, and our will becomes His will. Our will ought to be to do His will as Jesus prayed in the Garden of Gethsemane in **Luke 22:42 ESV:** *"Father, if you are willing, remove this cup from me. Nevertheless, not my will, but yours, be done."*

God works within us to do and to want to do His will and to do His good pleasure, *"for it is God who works in you, both to will and to work for his good pleasure,"* **Philippians 2:13 ESV.** God's aim is for us to do His will and to desire His pleasure. He wants us to be one in Him. He wants our will and good pleasure to be in sync with His.

The last part of this familiar and encouraging passage of Scripture in **Ephesians 3:20 ESV** says: *"Now to him who is able to do far more abundantly than all that we ask or think, according to the power at work within us."* This verse is given a greater understanding, I believe, in Eugene Peterson's paraphrase, **The Message**: *"God can do anything, you know – far more than you could ever*

203

*imagine or guess or request in your wildest dreams! He does it not by pushing us around but by working within us, his Spirit deeply and gently within us."*

When we have achieved an understanding of His will for us and get involved in actually doing His will, we soon discover Satan pushing hard against us in doing God's will. At this point, we must just arm ourselves in God's provision and stand positioned in the power and might of God.

So, don't worry about the pushing. Pushing is going to happen; just stand in God's might. You are held in position with His hand. Stand and watch God work and show His love, confidence, and peace. *"Watch what God does, and then you do it, like children who learn proper behavior from their parents. Mostly what God does is love you. Keep company with him and learn a life of love. Observe how Christ loved us. His love was not cautious but extravagant. He didn't love in order to get something from us but to give everything of himself to us. Love like that."* **Ephesians 5:1-2 MSG**

As God positions you, He makes provisions for you, and protects you at the position He has placed you, so play your position. Don't be surprised when you are pushed. Expect it.

Think about it. *Selah!*

## Day 82: The Big Lie

*"We are careful to be honorable before the Lord, but we also want everyone else to see that we are honorable."* **2 Corinthians 8:21 NLT**

To be careful to tell the truth is not a value that we are taught much today. We are taught to get all you can from life and to not allow another to get the best of you. To lie or to steal is not bad. Just don't get caught is the major thing; that's what is bad.

We want to be first. We want to get the best. We want to hold on to the best. We want to take all the advantages in life, to get it while the getting is good, and on and on it goes. To be careful to be honorable is not a value that is sought. To be honorable might require that we forfeit our position, settle for less, look after another, or give what we have to a less fortunate person.

Being honest and honorable may not even be anywhere on our list. But that is what God desires us to be, honest and honorable before Him and everyone else. We have fallen victim to a false set of values that are a lie from Satan, the father of all lies. Jesus commented about Satan in **John 8:44 ESV:** *"You are of your father the devil, and your will is to do your father's desires. He was a murderer from the beginning, and does not stand in the truth, because there is no truth in him. When he lies, he speaks out of his own character, for he is a liar and the father of lies."* Jesus, in contrast, is truth. In **John 14:6 KJV,** Jesus says that He is *". . . the way, the truth, and the life."*

When we become a new creation in Christ Jesus, we begin to change our natural inclinations and works of the flesh to spiritual fruits of righteousness, **Galatians 5:16-25.** Lying is as natural to mankind as the truth is to God. In **Numbers 23:19 ESV,** we read: *"God is not man, that he should lie, or a son of man, that he should change his mind. Has he said, and will he not do it? Or has he spoken, and will he not fulfill it?"*

God wants us to be as one with Him as He and His Son are one. We are to turn from human, sinful traits to the righteousness of Jesus. We are new creations and need to learn to live like the new creation.

What is a lie? A lie is something that is not the truth and the total truth. The truth has not just a shade of veracity, but it is open and totally exposed without concern. For some reason we have fallen victim to the idea that there are little white lies, or lies that are "not quite the truth." That is the biggest lie of all. Don't fall for it, and don't accept it. Just reject it and seek to be honest before all. The truth makes life much more simple. Mark Twain has said; *"If you tell the truth, you don't have to remember anything."*

One day all of mankind will stand before the Truth, the Way and the Life, and we will have to give an account of the way we conducted our life. *"And no creature is hidden from his sight, but all are naked and exposed to the eyes of him to whom we must give account."* **Hebrews 4:13 ESV**

Don't fall for the lie; bow before the Truth.

Think about it. *Selah!*

## Day 83: For The Glory Of God

*"And whatever you do or say, do it as a representative of the Lord Jesus, giving thanks through him to God the Father."* **Colossians 3:17 NLT**

That God would use whatever we do for the good should be the reason we do anything. Every thought, every deed, and every effort of each day of our lives ought to be done for the glory of God.

In his book **"All of Grace,"** Charles Spurgeon, who is often referred to as the "Prince of Preachers," wrote: *"Who knows how many will find their way to peace by what they read here? A more important question to you, dear reader, is this: Will you be one of them?"* I, too, have no clue as to who will read any book that I may write, but I wish to honor and glorify God in what I write and help to bring about a clearer understanding of God's working in our lives and the relationship of God's Word to life.

Spurgeon tells this story: *"A certain man who placed a fountain by the wayside, hung a cup near to it by a little chain. He was told some time after that a great art critic had found much fault with the design sign of the fountain. His response to the bearer of the news was: 'Do many thirsty persons drink at it?' The resounding answer was that thousands of poor people, men, women, and children, had their thirst quenched at the fountain. The man smiled and said that he was little troubled by the critic's observation, only he hoped that on some sultry summer's day the critic himself might fill the cup, and be refreshed, and praise the name of the Lord."*

Everyone ought to strive for excellence and do everything even beyond our own capability and into the capability of God and beyond our best and into the strong, capable arms of God. So, if God gives you a desire that seems to be beyond you, then seek that desire. Don't be satisfied with what you are capable of doing, but put your confidence into what God is capable of doing, and then stand back and be amazed and witness everyone else standing in amazement.

I close with a poetical line of Spurgeon:

*Here is my fountain,*
*Here is my cup:*
*Find fault if you please,*
*But do drink from the cup.*
*Do drink from the water of life!*

Think about it. *Selah!*

## Day 84:  Hey!  This Is My Church!

*"And I tell you, you are Peter, and on this rock I will build my church, and the gates of hell shall not prevail against it."* **Matthew 16:18 ESV**

Those are powerful words. Not even Satan and all his angels are capable of conquering the church that Jesus built.  Strangely enough, right after this statement we find Peter wanting to alter the foundation of Jesus' church by saying: *" 'Heaven forbid, Lord,' he said, 'This will never happen to you!' Jesus turned to Peter and said, 'Get away from me, Satan!  You are a dangerous trap to me. You are seeing things merely from a human point of view, not from God's.' "* **Matthew 16:22-23  NLT**

Peter thought he was defending Jesus, but Jesus needed no defending.  He was on the offensive.  Jesus was in the process of building His church at that very moment.  We are that church; we are His people, the sheep of His pasture.

You might get mad at Peter, but the same thing happens all the time today.  Have you ever gotten mad because you didn't like the way things were going in "your church?"  There is a good chance that "your church" has had a split, a fight or a division within it. Have you ever heard someone say, *"Well, if you don't like the way we do things in our church, then find yourself another one"?*  I have.

What am I saying?  I'm saying that if you consider the place where you attend as your church, then it is not Jesus' church.  He does not bless the gathering of people to do things the way they like it.  He blesses His church and those who worship Him within His church. It is that church that the gates of hell cannot conquer. ISIS can't, Communism can't, intellectualism can't, religions can't, philosophers and their philosophy can't, and Satan himself in all his power cannot. Jesus' church will stand and will last throughout eternity.

Do you belong to Jesus' Church? If you do, you will notice that the fruit of the Spirit thrives there, the love of God abides there, and the glory of God resides there. People are happy there, people are saved there, people are encouraged there, people are blessed there, and everyone is welcomed there.

Where the Spirit of the Lord is, it is there that we find freedom, liberty, and peace. **2 Corinthians 3:17**

Think about it. *Selah!*

## Day 85: And The Winner Is!

*"If you are a thief, quit stealing. Instead, use your hands for good hard work, and then give generously to others in need."* **Ephesians 4:28 NLT**

When I was in Bible College my friends and I would jokingly state this verse but change the punctuations. The King James Version reads it this way: *"Let him that stole steal no more: but rather let him labour, working with his hands the thing which is good, that he may have to give to him that needeth,"* **Ephesians 4:28 KJV.** The way we would state it is like this: *"Let him that stole, steal; no more let him labour, working with his hands, this thing is good."*

I thought it was a bit funny at the time, but it is quite applicable to the mindset of our world today. We say: *"Get all you can and can all you get; he who dies with the most toys wins; and don't work hard, work smart."* Paul tells us here that we should be diligent to work hard in order that we might give to the needs of others. Not only should we give but give generously. This is in stark contrast to what our world insists that we do. Things of value are acquired through work.

Luke writes in **Acts 20:35 KJV** where Paul encourages the early believers to live as Jesus taught: *"It is more blessed to give than to receive."* Our reason for working is in order that we might be able to give to others.

David Jeremiah tells of a story that a grandmother in his church shared with him about her grandchild. The children's ministry there was having the children fill jars with coins to give to a certain mission field to help buy some supplies for the poor children of their area. She noticed her grandson's jar had a five-dollar bill in it. It was his monthly allowance. She inquired of her grandson as to why he had put his whole allowance in the jar. He told her, "Well, the children over there are in great need and I wanted to help them. All I would do would be to buy another toy." Wow! Give it all, give generously, and give extravagantly. God loves a cheerful giver.

The winner is not the collector; the winner is the giver.

One of my favorite hymns is "Give of Your Best to the Master" by Howard B Grose:

*"Give of your best to the Master,*
*Give of the strength of your youth;*
*Throw you soul's fresh glowing ardor,* (a warm and burning emotion)
*Into the battle for truth.*

*Jesus has set the example -*
*Daunt-less was He, young and brave;*
*Give Him your loyal devotion,*
*Give Him the best that you have."*

Give freely and generously, give with an open hand, hold nothing back, and give with a gracious, loving, and open heart. Give joyfully to the Lord.

Think about it. *Selah!*

## Day 86: What Is The Real Number?

*"So when all these things begin to happen, stand and look up, for your salvation is near!"* **Luke 21:28 NLT**

The news is that Christians are dropping in number. Those who are attending our churches today are becoming fewer and fewer, as the polls are revealing. That may not be exactly a true statement. It could be that the number of "actual" Christians is just now being made known.

A friend of mine informed me of a comment of Ed Stetzer on the subject, who put it this way: *"Christianity is not dying, as I've often said; nominal Christianity is."* My friend went on to say: *"The nominals are now declaring their "nothing" belief system. But Pew reports that the committed are remaining strong. There's a redefining of "Christian" in our country. So, I agree with you; we are just now recognizing "actual" Christianity."*

I believe that it was Mark Twain who said: *"It doesn't take much to be a Christian, but it does take all of him."* Well, that is true. We must count the cost and give all. *"If you want to be my disciple, you must hate everyone else by comparison—your father and mother, wife and children, brothers and sisters—yes, even your own life. Otherwise, you cannot be my disciple.* **Luke 14:26 NLT**

What about you? Are you a nominal Christian or a real Christian? Are you giving your all, the total you? The time is now at hand that we who are "actual" Christians need to become even more dedicated and active in the spreading of the Good News. Are you included in the real number?

Think about it. *Selah!*

## Day 87: Some Things God Cannot Do

*" . . . 'I will remember their sins and their lawless deeds no more.' Where there is forgiveness of these, here is no longer any offering for sin."*
**Hebrews 10:17-18 ESV**

God can do anything but there are some things he chooses not to do. For these things we should be grateful for we are greatly blessed.

- **God cannot lie to his children.**

**Numbers 23:19 NLT:** *"God is not a man, so he does not lie. He is not human, so he does not change his mind. Has he ever spoken and failed to act? Has he ever promised and not carried it through?"*

- **God cannot turn his back on his children.**

**Deuteronomy 7:9 NLT** *"Understand, therefore, that the Lord your God is indeed God. He is the faithful God who keeps his covenant for a thousand generations and lavishes his unfailing love on those who love him and obey his commands."*

- **He cannot see the sins of his children that have been covered by the blood of his Son Jesus.**

**Psalm 103:10-12** *"He has not punished us for all our sins; nor does he deal harshly with us, as we deserve. For his unfailing love toward those who fear him is as great as* the height of the heavens above the earth. He has removed our sins as far from us as the east is from the west."

**Isaiah 38:17b ESV** ". . . you have cast all my sins behind your back."

God cannot sin against Himself, and He only does that which He pleases. Aren't you glad that God has limited Himself out of His great love for us?

Think about it? *Selah!*

## Day 88:  Don't Let Success Defeat You

*"Then Jesus was led up by the Spirit into the wilderness to be tempted by the devil."* **Matthew 4:1 ESV**

Everyone desires to be successful, but not everyone has the determination to do what it takes to be successful.  With success comes trial.  Oswald Chambers has said: *"All efforts of worth and excellence are difficult."*  That is true but with having attained success and having achieved our desired point of worth and excellence come even greater difficulties.  At that point, it is "tempting" to let our guard down.

After the baptism of Jesus by John the Baptist and the audible announcement by the Father that "This is my beloved Son, with whom I am well pleased," **Matthew 3:17 ESV,** Jesus was led "by the Holy Spirit" into the wilderness for the expressed purpose of the Father, to be tempted.

Believers and most certainly leaders in the spreading of the Good News will be led by the Holy Spirit to be tempted, tried, and tested.  The third temptation was where Satan took Jesus up to a very high mountain to show him all the kingdoms of the world and their glory and said: *"All these I will give you, if you will fall down and worship me,"* **Matthew 4:9**.  It was as if Satan were saying, "You don't have to go through all the pain to achieve the Father's plan.  I'll give them to you.  Isn't that much easier?"

Watch out for praise directed toward you because of how wonderful and successful you are.  You will be tempted to take short cuts, to think it's all about you and begin to be proud of what you have accomplished. *"It is God who works in you both to will and to do for His good pleasure,"* **Philippians 2:13**, and He is the one who has brought all of this to fruition. He deserves all the glory and praises, not us.

Don't let success defeat you. Remember whose you are and who it is that gives you strength. It is in your weakness that you have been made strong. Your strength will only defeat you.

Think about it. *Selah!*

## Day 89:  A Private Get-A-Way

*"And he said to them 'Come away by yourselves to a desolate place and rest awhile.' For many were coming and going, and they had no leisure even to eat."*
**Mark 6:31 ESV**

We hear often of the joy of having "our own little private get-a-way." A get-a-way is a place to recoup, rest, and relax.  Mark records a time when Jesus took His disciples away from the crowd where they could be alone, talk and communicate with each other.  We often read in the Bible where Jesus, Himself, would retreat to a solitary or desolate place to pray where there were no distractions, and He could meditate and talk with his Father in heaven.

Today we need times for meditation, prayer, and allowing God to speak with us.  It is not just a retreat; it is a necessity.

Richard Baxter was an Anglican chaplain to the king during England's Civil War.  He then left the Church of England to become a leader of the Nonconformists Movement.  He wrote the following about the need of the Christian to retreat to a solitary place in which to pray:

*"Our spirits need every help, and to be freed from every hindrance in the work.  If, in private prayer, Christ directs us to 'enter into our closet and shut the door, that our Father may see us in secret,' so should we do this in meditation?  How often did Christ himself retire to some mountain, or wilderness, or other solitary place!  I give not this advice for occasional meditation, but for that which is set and solemn.  Therefore withdraw yourself from all*

*society, even that of godly men, that you may awhile enjoy the society of your Lord. If a student cannot study in a crowd, who exercises only his invention and memory, much less should you be in a crowd, who are to exercise all the powers of your soul, and upon an object so far above nature."*

Do you want God to speak to you? You need to get alone with Him and find a solitary place where there is no one but you and God. Think about Him, be quite, listen to Him, meditate upon His Word and His Word to you, and you will come out energized, informed, productive, and full of the wisdom and power of God.

*"Come away by yourselves . . ."* **Mark 6:31 ESV.**

Think about it. *Selah!*

# Day 90: You Are A Work Of Art

*"For we are God's masterpiece. He has created us anew in Christ Jesus, so we can do the good things he planned for us long ago."* **Ephesians 2:10 NLT**

Have you ever taken note of what God has done through you? Did you know that God has perfectly designed you and awesomely equipped you to bring glory to Him doing that which He has called you to do? Have you ever considered that there is no one else on the face of this earth that can successfully perform the mission that you have been called and equipped to do?

When you received Jesus Christ as your personal Savior, He placed in your heart a great desire to live for Him and to serve Him. You see, you are His masterpiece! He made you brand new; a new creation, something different from all other creations, a true work of art. You are His workmanship.

Here is the problem: As we serve God, we begin to see other creations of God, and we begin to think that they are better than we are, or that they are more useful than we are, and even more precious to God than we are. All those thoughts are a lie. They are a lie from the mind of Satan himself. He has caused you to covet the gift or the place of someone else. You are exhibiting a desire for vainglory, or misdirected glory. To God be the glory, not to another and certainly not to me.

One of the early church fathers, Thomas A' Kempis, wrote in his The Imitation of Christ, *"The saints who are highest in God's sight are the least in their own; and the more glorious they are, the more humble they are in heart, full of truth and heavenly joy and not desirous of vainglory."*

May I offer to you a few personal desires in which you ought to aim?

Be all that God has called you to be, not to that which He has called someone else to be.

Be all you can be right where you are, where God has placed you, not where God has placed someone else.

Be all you can be with the perfect equipment that God has equipped you with, not with the equipment that God has equipped someone else.

Place your eyes on God and engage in the calling that He has called you and don't question your effectiveness. Be a faithful servant and you will be totally effective in your ministry.

*"Do not be slothful in zeal, be fervent in spirit, serve the Lord."* **Romans 12:11 ESV**

Think about it. *Selah!*

**Other books written by this author.**

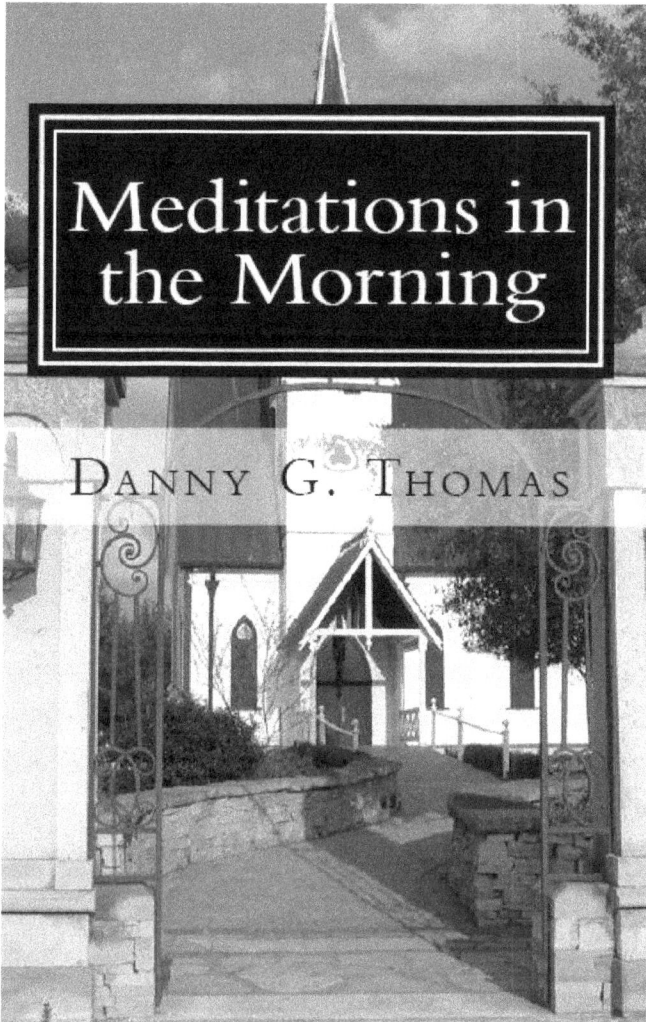

Meditations in
the Morning

DANNY G. THOMAS

# The Search: For Wisdom and Understanding

Danny G. Thomas

The Quest:
For Strength
and Knowledge

Danny G. Thomas

www.ingramcontent.com/pod-product-compliance
Lightning Source LLC
Chambersburg PA
CBHW060920040426
42445CB00011B/718